Praise for
How to be an Amazing Teacher

Caroline Bentley-Davies has produced a significant resource to support teachers in reviewing and reflecting on their professional practice. Her approach is authoritative and practical and she explores in a detailed and systematic manner the incredibly complex range of variables that enable effective learning. Her focus on reflection in practice is particularly welcome and she provides a range of resources to encourage teachers to become more aware and robust about their own teaching. Her insights and examples ensure that this will be a highly credible and relevant resource for teachers committed to supporting and enabling effective learning.

John West-Burnham, Professor of Educational Leadership
St Mary's University College

How to be an Amazing Teacher does what it says on the cover. Caroline has provided a lifelong teaching resource that will give new teachers tools and techniques that can be used immediately, as well as giving more established educators refreshing ideas and strategies to build off their own best practice.

Her writing style is a delightful balance between engaging personalisation and clear instruction and example. I have already used some of her ideas and intend to keep it on that special shelf of books that are well read and well used.

If you haven't got a copy, go and get one. If you have a copy, go and get one for someone else. They will thank you for it and so will their students.

Roy Leighton, educator, author and values consultant

Caroline captures the enthusiasm amazing teachers strive for, as well as all that is positive in this challenging and rewarding career. Full of highly practical suggestions and advice.

Sue Lane, Principal Teaching and Learning Consultant
Peterborough Local Authority

An extremely readable and practical guide, made particularly accessible and useful by the personal approach of an excellent practitioner.

Nicola Copitch, Secondary Lecturer in Teaching
University of Wolverhampton

A really valuable book for all teachers. This really made me reflect on my classroom skills again. I loved the section on 'student voice', which really focused on the students' experience in the classroom.

Kate Lewis, Advanced Skills Teacher
Arthur Mellows Village College

The value of this book is its focus on teaching and learning as a fundamentally interpersonal process in which dialogue and relationships are central rather than 'off the peg' techniques. Bentley-Davies presents a picture of teaching and learning as an invigoratingly open-ended voyage of reflective discovery which works best when pupils and teachers are in partnership and teachers are clear-sighted about their own strengths and development targets.

Carey Philpott, Head of the Centre for Excellence in Teacher Education, University of Strathclyde

Caroline Bentley-Davies provides a checklist of what outstanding teachers do that I wish I'd seen when I was getting started. The book is practical, uplifting and immensely reassuring. It reminds us that whilst brilliant teachers are awe-inspiring to watch, their skills are essentially learnable. Caroline Bentley-Davies' book provides a canny mix of advice and opportunities for reflection on the journey towards being an outstanding teacher. The style is eminently calm and practical.

Geoff Barton, Headteacher, King Edward VI School

This book jumps off the page from the very beginning, grabs you and never lets go. Every chapter is a gem. Each has excitement, ideas, tools. What's more, it covers the waterfront of everything that is key without ever getting bogged down. Caroline Bentley-Davies is Amazing. Read it as soon as you can if you want to appreciate and improve your teaching to gain maximum benefit.

Michael Fullan, Professor Emeritus, OISE/University of Toronto

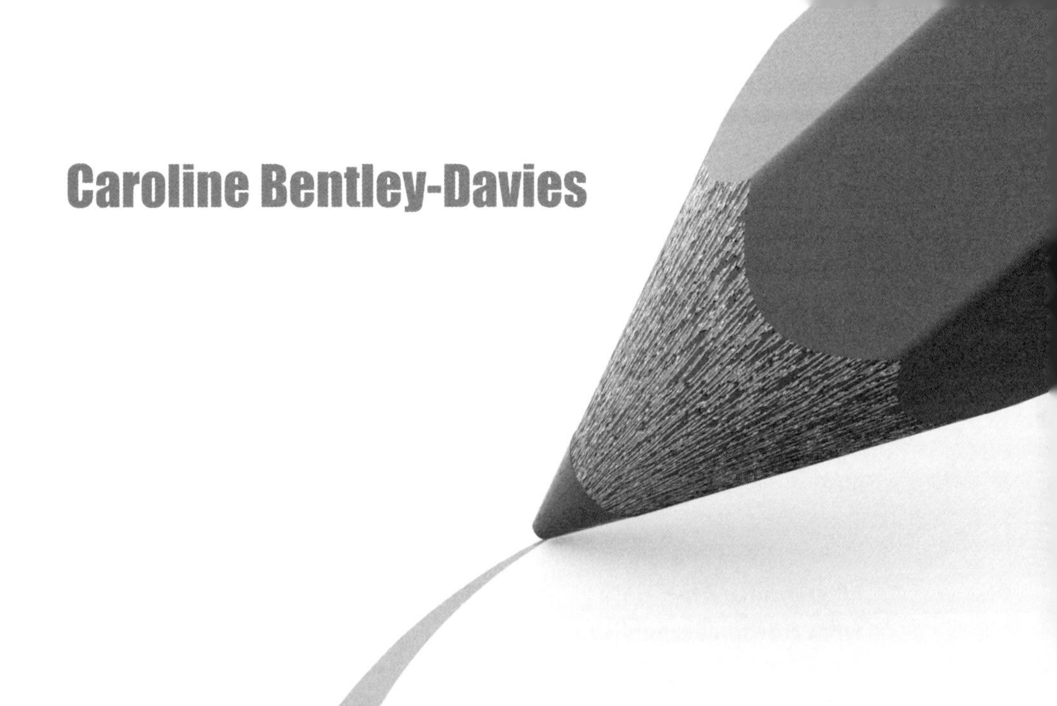

Caroline Bentley-Davies

How to be an Amazing Teacher

Crown House Publishing Ltd
www.crownhouse.co.uk
www.crownhousepublishing.com

First published by

Crown House Publishing Ltd
Crown Buildings, Bancyfelin, Carmarthen, Wales, SA33 5ND, UK
www.crownhouse.co.uk

and

Crown House Publishing Company LLC
6 Trowbridge Drive, Suite 5, Bethel, CT 06801, USA
www.crownhousepublishing.com

British Library of Cataloguing-in-Publication Data
A catalogue entry for this book is available
from the British Library.

10-digit ISBN 1845904427
13-digit ISBN 978-184590442-5

LCCN 2010927092

Printed and bound in the UK by
Bell and Bain Limited, Glasgow

With thanks to: Beverley Randell, Caroline Lenton and all of the Crown House team for their expertise and patience. Special thanks to Natalie Packer, consultant, for her expertise. A huge thank you to all of the teachers who generously shared their strategies for successful teaching, particularly many of the teachers at The Deepings School for giving me my very first experience of the power of Amazing teaching – most memorably Mrs Julie Chapman, Mr Gerry Cannings and Mrs V. Poletti. Finally, to my parents for developing my love of learning, and most importantly to my husband, Ross, for encouraging me to write this book in the first place.

Contents

Introduction

How to be an Amazing Teacher

In most people's school experience there was an amazing teacher: the teacher who changed their outlook on life, helped them to succeed and whose lessons will never be forgotten. Don't we all dream of being *that* teacher? Like all of us, I started my learning journey as a student. I was fortunate enough to have a great many good teachers and some that were really special. They had that 'amazing' quality which meant that at the end of their lessons we would look at our watches surprised that an hour had flown by so quickly. We were engrossed and fascinated by their lessons, but also by the skills they had in fostering and nurturing us as individuals, encouraging us to challenge ourselves and attempt the seemingly impossible.

The successful teachers (and yes there were some that certainly weren't, and I bet we've all had those!) seemed to make teaching appear relatively easy. They had a natural ease and humorous rapport with even the most difficult of classes (for one of my subjects I was in the second from bottom set – and in a traditional comprehensive, you can imagine that student behaviour could be challenging at times). It was only when I started teaching as a PGCE student myself that I realised that although we might think we have a natural aptitude for teaching – and the belief that some teachers are 'born and not made' – it really isn't that simple.

I have since watched thousands of teachers teach lessons in schools across the country, from the inner city to the country idyll. Some lessons have been truly outstanding; others nothing short of terrible (for a myriad of different reasons). What I will say is that from each and every one I have learnt something, whether it is a crucial aspect of lesson planning, the best way to create a learning environment or strategies to coax an excellent answer out of a nervous student. However, as educationalists we must believe that an individual's skills can be strengthened and improved – in ourselves as well as in those we teach.

My lessons were judged as outstanding when, as a young teacher of 23, the large comprehensive school I was teaching in was inspected. I was rather surprised by this as during the Ofsted inspection I had been teaching in the way I always had and in fact two students had been extremely disruptive in one of the lessons. I had dealt with them just as I would have done with any other disruptive student, so in some respects my behaviour management skills were outstanding – which allowed me to focus on the important job of teaching and learning in the lesson. However, other skills that an outstanding teacher possesses, such as the mastery of interpersonal skills, the ability to track and help students progress over the longer term and finally, but nonetheless importantly, the ability to make sure that everybody counts – including yourself – was a skill I did not finally master until much later as a head of department.

And I'm still learning! This book has been written because when I meet teachers or run INSET days they have a host of questions they want answered: What makes an outstanding teacher? How do I improve my skills? How can you get behaviour right? How can I motivate the students who don't seem to want to learn? These questions not only come from newly qualified teachers but also those with countless years of experience, and very often senior leaders in charge of the quality of teaching and learning in a school. This book attempts to answer some of the most pertinent questions by reference to my own diverse experience of teaching as well as my observations of amazing teachers and all those that span the spectrum, from good to bad.

As a teacher, I keep up with a wide range of my ex-students and, as those of you who have been teaching for more than a decade will know, sooner or later if you have had a positive impact on your students you will be contacted through Facebook, by email or even memorably the fruit and veg aisle of Sainsbury's: 'Miss, I've become a teacher and it's because of your lessons on photosynthesis / Charles I / *Macbeth* / equations!' What I didn't quite expect while meeting up with an ex-student, sipping coffee and tackling a huge slice of chocolate cake, was to be asked a huge range of questions about how to become 'the best teacher possible'. My protégé's pen was hopefully poised over her notebook. 'What I want is actual rock solid tips …' she urged. This book is the result.

How you use the book is up to you. However, there are a few guiding principles that underpin the way it has been written so understanding them will help you to get the most out of it. As you will realise on your quest to become an amazing teacher, learning is a dynamic process. Yes I know, like my ex-student you just want the failsafe guide to get the outstanding lesson judgement by Ofsted or know the top ten tips before you move on to your next job. You can certainly read the book like this: you will gain lots of tips and strategies to use in the classroom and it will provide food for thought and help you on your way.

However, learning is a process. To become an amazing teacher, for you, might involve changing some habits, learning some new skills or even (scary stuff) taking some risks. With this in mind, at key moments there are **thinking points**. The idea behind them is that this concept is really rather important and you may wish to pause and reflect on it for a while. They highlight a key issue and ask you: Do you agree? Is this the case for you? Is this the sort of behaviour or rapport we would see if we peeked into your classroom? It should make you think and, as we know, this is how the best learning takes place.

Similarly, at the end of most chapters there are **reflection moments**. These encourage you to note down for yourself: What are the three things that have helped you in this chapter? What has caused you to think? What might you want to try in your lessons or in your approaches with students? It also encourages you to record a couple of targets related to this area. As research has shown, writing down our intentions is a key way of ensuring that they happen. It provides not only a written reminder but a commitment to try out some strategies, thought processes or teaching techniques that you have decided might help you. Then of course it is up to you to make the effort to try them, evaluate them and if they work (and remember not everything works first time – you will need to practise) to add them to your repertoire. There is sufficient space in each section of the book for you to write these down on the page directly but should you prefer it, or if the copy belongs to the school's teaching and learning group, you may like to buy a small notebook and keep your intentions private. Either way, I do urge you to make a note of them.

It is possible to just dip into the book, particularly if you feel that an aspect of your teaching requires a boost and you have not got the time to read it through from beginning to end. Each section is a complete whole and it will make perfect sense if read in this way. Individual chapters likewise make good INSET reference material or are helpful as a way of improving one part of your practice.

However, the real intention was for the book to be read from start to finish. There is good sense in this, since it takes you on the journey of an amazing teacher. Section I looks at the key characteristics and skills of an amazing teacher and just as importantly students' perspectives on this (they are not always the same as teachers' views). Section II moves on to the practicalities or the 'nuts and bolts' of developing the skills of an amazing teacher, offering concrete strategies about aspects of lesson planning and delivery that can be readily translated into the classroom. Section III looks at some issues behind underachievement and the groups most usually affected by this: boys, special educational needs (SEN) students and surprisingly Gifted and Talented students. Finally, Section IV tackles some of the areas of teaching that can be problematic for all of us on occasion and deals with issues such as difficulties in the classroom, the need for positivity in dealings with students and the need for balance in our teaching lives.

This book is result of the thousands of questions, experiences and lessons. Keep open minded and try out some of the techniques described. Let me know what works for you – I'm always keen to know about your own tips and ideas that you think are worth sharing. Remember, like our students we are all still learning and it is the acceptance of this mindset and the willingness to take chances in developing new skills that sets us on the way to becoming an amazing teacher.

Enjoy!

Caroline Bentley-Davies
www.bentley-davies.co.uk

Section I

The Skills of an Amazing Teacher

Chapter 1

Why We Need to Foster the Skills of an Amazing Teacher

> For me, an outstanding teacher tries to put the fun back into learning; whilst never losing the focus that something challenging and worthwhile is being learnt.
>
> Sue Lane, senior secondary consultant, Peterborough ”

People decide to become teachers for a whole host of reasons. Some know from an early age that they have a vocation. Their desire to pass on information and instruct others can be overwhelming. Younger siblings and soft toys have been lined up and practised on from the tenderest of ages. For these individuals the road to teaching is well planned and rigorously signposted. Others come to it much later in life, deciding that the corporate world has a poverty of fulfilment, despite its obvious material trappings. Others are cast adrift on the sea of careers and eventually try teaching as one of many possible suitable choices, surprising themselves by enjoying and committing to a career they didn't visualise themselves ever undertaking. It doesn't matter how you decided to become a teacher; what matters is that you did and that while you are teaching you continually seek to become the best teacher you can. Sounds easy enough, doesn't it?

Watching an amazing teacher is like watching any specialist: they make it look effortless and straightforward when it fact it takes an immense amount of skill and split-second decision making to make it happen. An amazing teacher commands the complete attention of their class (not an easy task when thirty-one or more individuals have many more exciting activities on their minds). An amazing teacher notices and responds to students as individuals, noticing perhaps that Ian is rather quiet today, or that Millie isn't trying her hardest or that Michael lacks confidence with a particular task. An amazing teacher addresses these issues directly or makes a mental note to have a quiet word with the student or check with their form tutor so that barriers to learning are broken down. If you have been taught by an amazing teacher you will know what it is like to be encouraged, to be pushed, to be challenged and to feel supported that with their guidance you can achieve your very best.

Developing the skills of an amazing teacher takes time. It also takes effort and the ability to reflect and be honest about your performance and your qualities. Becoming an amazing teacher is not all about length of service. We have all experienced in many different areas of life the lacklustre individual who claims expertise or even 'excellence' purely because they have been doing the same job for over twenty years. But twenty years of doing the job isn't the same as twenty years of experience. It all depends on whether the individual has thought and reflected on what they have done – or whether they are just repeating the same year twenty times over.

The same is true in developing the skills and characteristics of an amazing teacher; we have to be willing to think and sometimes even rethink the way we go about something. Some amazing teachers are in their first few years of teaching. Some teachers have become amazing teachers after a much longer period. What is evident about all really exceptional teachers is that they *still* believe there is plenty left for them to learn and set about doing this.

In defining the essence of an amazing teacher I think it helps to think about the five Es: enthusiasm, expertise, empathy, empowerment and enterprise. These reflect the key attributes that an amazing teacher has in abundance. Developing and refining these skills takes time, hard work and commitment. You may feel that some of these come more naturally to you than others, but the ones you struggle with most are actually the ones to start with.

1. Enthusiasm

Whatever you are teaching – whether it is Maths, Modern Languages or making meringues – the key to getting your message across in a successful way is enthusiasm. An amazing teacher gets seriously excited about their subject. They find the finer points of their subject endlessly fascinating but most importantly they transfer that excitement to their students. Think about Gordon Ramsay for a moment: you only have to watch him give a cookery demonstration or guide a would-be chef to see him literally bouncing with enthusiasm as he discusses the ingredient or dish he is planning to cook.

So you have to be excited about whatever it is you are teaching. That seems straightforward enough, doesn't it? However, there are some areas of the curriculum which are rather demanding, difficult or just plain dull. The enthusiastic teacher realises this so puts effort and energy into finding creative, innovative ways to keep themselves and most importantly their charges interested about the topic.

I recently observed a Maths lesson in which I sat next to a rather sulky 14-year-old girl who I had met in the previous lesson where she had scowled, sulked and whispered her way throughout the entire period. In the Maths lesson she worked diligently and produced more work in ten minutes than she had done in the whole of the previous hour. When I implied that she seemed to enjoy Maths she dissented saying, 'No, I don't!' When I remonstrated that clearly she must like it since she was working much harder than she had in the previous lesson, she raised a scornful eyebrow and asked me to observe the teacher for a minute. 'The thing is,' she sighed, 'he's just *so* enthusiastic that even though I don't *like* Maths, you just find yourself trying, even if you don't want to.' Here was high praise indeed and the efforts of the enthusiastic teacher were plain to see. He was a highly engaging teacher in his sixties who had gone to great efforts to make his lesson interesting. It had pace, rigour and challenge. He most probably had taught this area of the curriculum a hundred times in his career. But what was most noticeable was his passion for numbers and the excitement with which he explained what they were going to be doing. Most importantly he became enthused and excited by the *students'* responses and *their* efforts rather than his own mathematical skills.

Enthusiasm really is infectious. It is in finding fresh ways to teach a topic or reignite your own enthusiasm when teaching *Macbeth* for the fifteenth time that is the challenge. We need to strive to be like that Maths teacher who, seemingly against their will, gets his students motivated and interested in the subject.

2. Expertise

Enthusiasm is incredibly important; it is the spark that lights the interest for a student in a topic and makes them focus on the lesson even when they'd rather be thinking about something or somebody else. However, enthusiasm on its own is never enough. Enthusiasm needs to be tempered by the rigour and effort of careful lesson planning and underpinned by the expertise of the specialist. An amazing teacher continually develops and enhances their expertise – even if they have a first class degree in that subject. If you are keen to develop your know-how then you will be constantly looking for different, unusual and more effective ways of teaching a skill or concept to your students.

Recently I was running a training course for newly qualified teachers (NQTs) and we were sharing the different ways we each had for teaching a similar concept. Everybody was reacting excitedly to each others' ideas, weighing them up, reflecting on them, asking questions and deciding whether or not this would be a useful technique for employing with their own students. At the end of the session we all had several new ideas that we were interested in trialling and even as the trainer (or supposed expert) I had learnt two new methods. It pays to be receptive, alert to new ideas, always honing our expertise.

This open attitude towards learning contrasted greatly with an observation by one NQT who commented that she couldn't understand her head of department's attitude. Apparently he didn't attend courses and when we asked why she explained that he had simply said that he had 'nothing more to learn about teaching his subject'. What an assertion! Obviously starting with excellent subject knowledge is a great benefit and nobody would dispute that having a good master's degree makes you an expert. However, developing expertise is a process not a destination – and we *all* need to develop our expertise.

Many subjects are still developing (think of all the amazing developments in science and ICT where breakthroughs are made every year and the technology behind your latest laptop becomes obsolete sometimes before you have even finished paying for it). Even if your subject of choice is medieval history, new research is always being published and even if the material is the same there are a myriad of new techniques, technologies and teaching ideas to discover, embed and enjoy. We owe it to ourselves to become experts in the subjects we are teaching. We need to become specialists in all the different ways and various strategies involved in teaching. We need to think carefully about developing further knowledge about parts of the curriculum we are less sure about and in continually enriching our skills. Would you really want to be taught by somebody who thought that they had already amassed a complete and extensive knowledge and had *nothing* more to learn? It is amazingly arrogant to believe that we have nothing further to learn. Interestingly the school in question soon received an Ofsted inspection and it was less of a surprise to see that the core subject lead by the supposed 'expert' who had nothing further to learn was singled out for severe criticism regarding the quality of his teaching.

An amazing teacher is *always* seeking to know more whether through research, further reading, training courses or through the observation of colleagues. They never reach that cosy feeling of self satisfaction whereby they think that they have learnt all there is to learn. They are constantly on the lookout for ways to develop their skills perhaps through training as an examiner, taking further study, reading the latest research or through information from their subject association. They have expertise, but they do not rest on their laurels. It is that constant questing and the awareness that they are still developing their skills that makes them really amazing.

In addition we must not forget the vital but seemingly hidden skills and expertise behind the process of developing classroom management skills, motivating our students and ensuring the well-being of the student in our care. These are all talents – and ones we overlook at our peril. It is important to have detailed subject and specialist knowledge, but unless this is harnessed with the ability to manage the sometimes turbulent and difficult classroom our efforts will be wasted.

3. Empathy

Amazing teachers have the ability to empathise with their students. They understand that for some or indeed many students learning is difficult, challenging or simply not enjoyable. In recognising this, they are able to perceive the barriers that an individual student faces and the ability to put themselves in their shoes. Although they have the capacity to sympathise and understand what it would be like to be the student, perhaps one who is experiencing a turbulent home life, they work with the student in a way that not only supports them but enables them to succeed. The ability to empathise does not give student a 'get-out clause' or a way of avoiding learning; the skill is in seeking to understand an individual's circumstances so you are best able to help them overcome the challenges they may be facing.

4. The ability to empower

The amazing teacher is not one who has the largest ego. In fact excellent teaching depends upon teachers who are able to support and then create enough independence within each student for them to manage alone. A good teacher realises that while they could be the 'star' of the lesson, really effective learning takes place when the teacher is not centre stage. This can be a difficult balancing act. True, students must feel they have sufficient support and guidance from their teacher so they can ask for help and develop their skills, but this does not mean creating an over-reliance or dependency upon the teacher. We must remember that true mastery of skill means that a student can demonstrate these *without* us hovering over them. In the examination hall or the wider arena of life they need to be able to competently and creatively apply all that we have taught them – without us there as a safety net.

It is often all too easy to fall victim to the urge to create a dependency on you as the expert. This can sometimes feel quite nice in the cosy classroom. However, constantly checking or rechecking work, looking up information or spellings for students who are perfectly capable of doing this for themselves or allowing yourself to over-guide or over-support students' work may actually be doing them less of a favour than you may think. Learning is challenging and as good teachers we should be working to make ourselves redundant. We should be teaching with the clear aim that students will be able to succeed without us. We need to critically review our classroom arrangements and think about what teaching techniques are most appropriate and how they create independence. Similarly we need to hold back from doing too much for our students. Over-careful correcting of work, for example, might show teacher diligence, but it can also create a sloppy approach with the student who fails to read through their work because they know that Miss will do it for them.

What other strategies could you employ to help foster your students' independence? Thinking carefully about whether the groupings for work are the most appropriate for the task is crucial in empowering students. Some students over-rely on their neighbour when all pair work inevitably ends up with them working with the person sitting next to them. Deciding on the suitable groupings and whether to allow students to work in pairs or individually takes skill, but is important in developing individuals who are empowered to learn for themselves.

5. **Enterprising**

Last but by no means least is the enterprising spirit. An amazing teacher needs to develop this important facet of their personality. Skilful teaching is well planned and well resourced (and requires plenty of effort, another E) but amazing teachers are also enterprising as they spot opportunities for making links across the curriculum, finding exciting resources or different ways to engage learners with the dullest part of the curriculum.

The enterprising mindset is an important skill to foster – it helps you to rally when you realise you have left your lesson plan on the kitchen table and you will have to rapidly improvise using just your memory and twelve packets of coloured pencils! An enterprising teacher doesn't just see a photograph; they see fifteen different opportunities for using that object as an exciting resource. They don't despair when the DVD player is broken and their lesson is devised around showing a film; they have the ability to use creativity and ingenuity when situations go awry or when an unusual approach is needed.

Reflection moment

So how are your five Es? Which of the characteristics do you think you have most experience of? Make a note of these now. Which characteristics do you think you could do with a little enhancement in? Take the following light-hearted assessment which will help you identify your areas of strength and give you some possible ideas for improvement. Compare your 'gut feeling' with the results of the questionnaire below. If you are after a more objective view complete this with a colleague who will be able to advise you if they think you are giving really honest answers.

Questionnaire: What is your core E strength?

The following questionnaire is designed to help you to understand how our responses to situations and attitudes match the five Es. For each of the questions, try to imagine the situation that is being described and choose the answer that would be your most frequent response. Consider your response to each question, mark the most likely response with two marks and deduct two marks for the least likely response.

1. You have been asked to teach a new unit for A-Level and although you studied it at university you have not got any appropriate teaching resources for it. Do you:

a. See this as an excellent opportunity to develop some exciting new resources.
b. Know you have the subject expertise but use the internet and publishers to find suitable resources.
c. Understand that somebody needs to teach something new and this time it's you.
d. Make sure you read up on it but design investigative lessons whereby the students will also be teaching each other.
e. See this as a good opportunity to see what other schools are doing and contact local teachers who are teaching the same unit.

2. After being taught by you for a year students are most likely to say:

a. 'Miss/Sir gets so excited about what they're teaching – they even jump about when explaining stuff!'
b. 'Miss/Sir really knows their stuff.'
c. 'Miss/Sir really helped me and understood me as a person.'
d. 'After their lessons I feel so much more confident and can do this for myself now.'
e. 'Can you remember the time when the experiment went wrong but Miss just carried on using her tights and Susie's pencil case?'

3. In lessons you get really excited about what you are teaching:

a. Every day, every topic. You can find something exciting about most things.
b. When you are teaching something you have a particular specialist interest in.
c. When you feel that you are really getting through to the students.
d. When the group work you have set up works really well and students can tell you what they learnt.
e. When you are forced to think on your feet and adapt to changing situations.

4. A television programme about the topic you have been teaching is being shown tonight. Do you:

a. Record it so you can watch it with your class at lunchtime.
b. Have seen it before and know that a few factual details are wrong.
c. Know that your students won't bother to watch it so show a short version of the highlights at the start of next lesson.
d. Use the idea of it to get students doing their own recorded presentations on a topic.
e. Ask students to watch it as homework and then ask those who have seen it to feedback the key points to others.

5. In lessons you are most likely to be heard saying:

a. 'This is *so* exciting. You are really going to love this.'
b. 'Not many people know this but actually . . .'

c. 'You think you might find this hard, but I know you, you *can* do this.'
d. 'I want you to think about this for two minutes in pairs before we all discuss it.'
e. 'I have just had a good idea. Why don't we . . . ?'

6. Your best recent lesson was one where:

a. You tried out a new way of explaining a topic and some exciting new group work techniques and it worked amazingly well.
b. You were able to show your expert knowledge.
c. You felt that all students joined in, even though you had to really boost their confidence for them to do so.
d. The students' feedback on their projects was so impressive.
e. One that didn't go according to plan – you had to adapt quickly but the students made really good progress.

7. When other people observe your lesson for the first time, they are likely to say:

a. 'Where do you find your energy from? You are so keen and lively.'
b. 'You know your stuff really well. I never knew that . . .'
c. 'I like the way you encouraged Ryan and your classroom climate is really great.'
d. 'I was impressed by how much the students achieved and their independence.'
e. I've got some really good new teaching strategies in mind after seeing that.'

8. Your comments in students' books have plenty of:

a. Positive praise and encouragement.
b. Corrections relating to factual errors.
c. Comments that build good relationships between you and the individual.
d. Comments that show the students where they have made mistakes – and demonstrates that they have taken steps to correct this.
e. A range of marking, including peer-assessment, self-assessment and useful charts showing progress.

9. You enjoy teaching because:

a. It is your passion and you want to achieve the best you can.
b. You love your subject and want to pass this on.
c. You enjoy working with the students and you really want to help them.
d. You enjoy seeing the students make progress with their learning.
e. Each and every day is different and unexpected.

10. One thing you think you need to be careful about is:

a. Wearing yourself out physically – you do bounce around a lot in lessons.
b. Talking too much about your pet interest and getting distracted by it.
c. Being a bit 'soft' with some students and not enforcing all the school rules.
d. Letting the students take over the lesson too much.
e. Your own organisation and ensuring you manage to cover everything in the specification on time.

Tot up the marks for each question. You will see how your answers broadly relate to the five different Es. Answer A = Enthusiasm, Answer B = Expertise, Answer C = Empathy, Answer D = Empower, and Answer E = Enterprising.

Reflection moment

Do your answers appear to suggest one dominating E? If so flip back and read the description of that skill. It is clearly an important skill to have, but it is important to foster all of the Es to balance your skills. An amazing teacher would expect to have answers that ranged across the different Es. Now look at which Es your answers really didn't match. Was there one area that was not matched much at all? These might be areas to focus on first. Use the description of this E to give you some pointers about addressing the balance. Remember, it is important to develop a range of skills so you can call on them when they are most appropriate and become a really amazing, well-rounded teacher.

Chapter 2

What Do Students Really Want from their Teachers?

It is all very well deciding you are going to be an amazing teacher. Yes, you've got the skills, and you've made a mental note to work on those areas that aren't quite there yet. But all in all you think you are pretty good – right? Well perhaps we are forgetting somebody in all of this. Our perception of ourselves can sometimes be very different to how others see us. We may *think* we possess all the relevant skills and that we are the most amazingly enterprising, enthusiastic and expert teacher, but what is the reality in our classroom? How do our students perceive us and more importantly how does what we do shape their experience in the classroom?

We forget the students at our peril. After all they are the sole reason for our presence. A skilled teacher always tries to be aware of how they are influencing the lesson and how the students are responding – or not. I say 'tries' deliberately as the ability to self-evaluate in the classroom and recognise our impact on students is notoriously difficult. It can be very easy to become caught up in the spirit of the lesson – perhaps even enjoying it so much *ourselves* that we become unaware that student participation has stopped or that you lost the class several minutes earlier.

In this chapter we will be considering strategies for developing a better awareness of what our students think of our teaching skills and strategies. Firstly, we will be considering how and when we ask them for their views.

The positives and perils of student voice

'Student voice' – asking for student responses to what they have been taught – is very common now and rightly so. However, this is often done at whole school or department level. This is useful but can sometimes give just a broad snapshot or impression about a subject or the quality of teaching. It is much more interesting, and potentially transformational, to actually undertake some student level reviews with individual classes. If you ask the right questions, instead of bland generalisations about a subject, you may receive some incisive and helpful gems about your own teaching – what students like and find useful. But be warned: although you may find that some of your ideas and thoughts about your teaching will be validated, you will certainly find out what students don't like as well. However, used in the right way this can be exceptionally useful. Any outstanding practitioner ought to be able to take constructive criticism – even if it stings at first.

When I took on my first meaty leadership role, I decided to sample the views of some of my students before I investigated the views of students across the department. Student voice wasn't well established in the school then and my Year 9 class were absolutely delighted and amazed to be actually asked for their opinions and took the responsibility very seriously. One of them wrote: 'Nobody has ever asked me what I thought about lessons before. This is great . . . now I get the chance to *tell all* . . .' Although it is now more common for students to be interviewed and asked to share their ideas, they still enjoy the opportunity to reveal how they feel about things.

There are a few points to bear in mind when asking for students' views. Like all of us, students will modify what they write if they have to 'own' the comments and include their names. Consider very carefully if you want an honest response (and what is the point of the exercise if you don't?) whether it is best to allow students to complete it anonymously, and what might be the best way of going about this. My experience indicates that asking questions relating to particular areas of the curriculum or aspects you have been teaching yield the richest responses. Therefore asking: 'What topic did you enjoy most this term and why?' is likely to lead to a more meaningful answer focused on teaching techniques rather than an open question such as, 'What do you like about my teaching?'

When writing questions try to avoid being too leading in the phrasing. It is a good idea to give students enough space to provide details and be aware that they might think of things you have not considered. It is important therefore not to give all the options or answers in a questionnaire (e.g. What would help you revise better for examinations? (a) Revision guides, (b) List of websites, (c) More examples of students' work or (d) More past papers). These are all good possibilities but they do not give the students any opportunity to add their own ideas – and you are trying to tap into their unique insight. They might have a better suggestion for the best way to help them revise, for example, so give them the opportunity to say so – even if the answer is unexpected or difficult to handle. How might you respond if the student as a free response wrote, 'I don't know the topic well enough – it needs to be re-taught first'. Anger: 'I've taught them this once already – don't they listen!' Despair: 'Oh God, there's only three weeks to go and now they are saying they don't know it.' Or would you think: 'Good, that student is being honest and I need to look again at teaching that topic in a different way, perhaps finding out what it was about it that they think they don't understand'?

Would your attitude and actions be different if it was one student out of thirty who responded that way, or twenty-eight out of thirty? It might be. Perhaps one student hasn't quite 'got it' and needs individual help, or maybe they are actually being 'brave' and highlighting an issue that many students experience. Either way when you get more than a handful of students saying the same thing it is certainly time to review the way you do things.

With my own students I was often intrigued by some of their responses. They were a very bright and articulate class who responded at length to some of the questions. One of the issues I found most interesting was when I asked them to rank order the topics they had enjoyed that year. I felt absolutely certain that the Shakespeare play would be the most loathed and also the most challenging; it was difficult, it was many students' first experience of the bard and had been greeted with howls of 'boring!' even before we started (just one example of the barrier created by students' preconceptions of some 'difficult' topics). However, it was unanimously the most popular; possibly because we had 'acted it out' and had done various different and unusual activities to bring it to life. I was dumbfounded.

It was equally interesting, although a tad disappointing, to find out that the novel which I had taught many times before and had complete confidence would be in the top three was far from a favourite. Looking at some of the comments I realised why. I had expected students to find Shakespeare dull and I had worked exceptionally hard to make the lessons lively and the resources interesting. I had strained to think of inventive ways of teaching it that would engage them and make it memorable. With the novel, I had over-relied upon past teaching experience and tailored the lessons less to the students' needs, expecting that past successes with other classes would carry me through.

This exercise was an interesting lesson for me but it was also useful in giving me insight into what was working and what wasn't. My class had experienced more success and enjoyment with something that was very difficult, but the need to think carefully about some 'old favourites' and schemes of work that might have served me well in the past but were due for a bit of a refresh – useful findings indeed.

Thinking point

Think carefully about asking for students' views – what is it you want to know? Be careful that you aren't just seeking confirmation for things you already know are successes and be open minded enough to allow the students scope to give you genuine comments. Think about what feedback you will give to the students – it might be worth sharing a few of your findings, particularly if you have asked them to rank order topics. Be aware also that if a number of students have identified something that needs attention – whether it is that they don't receive prompt enough marking, sufficient praise or a not enough variety of teaching techniques – you do need to take action. Even if the findings make uncomfortable reading at first, when you are on the quest to become an amazing teacher you must realise that sometimes you need to take on board the views of others – most importantly your students.

Reflection moment

- What questions would you really like to ask your students?

- How will you organise it? Do you think a questionnaire is appropriate? It has benefits because you can sample a large number of students (e.g. a whole class) but it has drawbacks as you can't always probe their answers or encourage those that don't want to add detail.

- If you ask students to discuss topics or questions in groups make sure you don't try to press a response on them (I sat in on an interview once where a teacher asked, 'But *which* bit in Drama is your absolute favourite bit?'). Also bear in mind that students may be less likely to offer you their honest evaluation if they are doing this directly to your face. Consider asking another teacher to interview your students and offer a similar return favour. It is often easier to be objective when it is not your curriculum or lessons under review.

- Finally, think about when you want to ask your students for their response. While it might be tempting to wait until the end of the year you are likely to be better able to use the feedback to improve your practice if you make this a common and regular part of your self-review – perhaps after a monthly topic or at periodic intervals.

Three things I would like to ask my students:

1.

2.

3.

When do I think it would be most profitable to do this?

Take a look at the questions below that one head of department devised to ask students in her subject area when investigating the area of revision. How do you think they reacted? How do you think yours would react? What responses do you think they would give? Why not ask them and find out – you might be quite surprised.

Questions to ask students about revision

1. What do you enjoy most about your lessons in . . .?
2. Which topic or area of study do you think you have been most successful with? Why do you think this was?
3. What grade are you aiming for?
4. Do you know what skills you have to show to achieve this grade?
5. What helps you improve in lessons?
6. Tell me about revision and your experience of the mocks. What helped you? What could be made better? How do you revise?
7. How much time do you spend on coursework? Do you spend as much time preparing for the examination?
8. Can you name three things that have helped you improve your work over the last year?

9. Do your parents/carers know how well you are doing?

10. Do you receive any guidance with your work from them? What would help you?

11. What specific things could be done by the school to help you do better in your exams?

12. What could you do to help you achieve?

Below is a different set of statements used in a semi-structured interview where the teacher discussed the questions with groups of six students from a variety of classes. After completing a few of these group interviews you will have a good amount of information and a clear indication of strengths and any areas for further investigation. It is of course possible to use these as a basis for a large scale questionnaire.

Statements for discussion of students' experiences in a particular subject

1. I think that I am improving in Science.

2. I enjoy my Science lessons.

3. I find Science lessons easier/the same/more challenging than other subjects.

4. I have a good knowledge and understanding of . . . (include key aspects from the curriculum that have recently been taught).

5. The teacher helps me improve when they ...

6. I often answer questions and participate in lessons.

7. Discipline is good in lessons.

8. The lessons encourage me to think for myself.

9. I find homework useful and complete it to the best of my ability.

10. The one thing that would help me improve further in Science would be ...

What characteristics do students want and value in their teacher?

> If you notice that a student is finding something too easy, then have the confidence to set them something else which is different and rethink your plans . . . teaching style also has a massive effect on the level of cooperation you will receive from a student . . . I guess that much of this stems from the teacher's own enthusiasm. Many teachers have become despondent; this attitude is bound to rub off on their students . . . Enthusiasm really is infectious, students will feed off it and (you) the teacher will benefit from their subsequent passion for the subject.
>
> Dan Coventry, ex-student

It is interesting to consider what wider characteristics students value in their teachers. Is it the ability to know the latest trends and to be 'down with the kids'? Is it better to be a bit slack about setting homework if you want to stay the right side of your students? Interviewing a number of students in Year 9 gave me some advice that I found very insightful. It seems that most students rate fairness, teaching expertise and a sense of humour higher than any other qualities. While many students might joke about wanting a 'soft' teacher or mutter gleefully that Mrs Caker can't 'control us', they really do know when they are being well taught and don't actually want to waste time in 'doss' lessons. They rate teaching expertise: teachers who know their job and can do it successfully. For students this means interesting them in the topic, keeping lessons varied and knowing a great deal about the subject, but most importantly having the skill and the ability to pass it on in an interesting way.

Fairness is another interesting concept and students were scathing about teachers who were thought to be unfair or who deviated too much from the concept of equal treatment for all. Probably all of us at some time or another have experienced favouritism in the home, classroom or work environment. In fact discussing issues like this with adults can create quite animated dialogue as lack of fair treatment (although sometimes this is only a perception) can still give rise to great emotion even years later. We need to strive to treat students justly. I say 'strive' because it can sometimes be very difficult. Some students are undoubtedly more likeable than others; some are always in trouble and do their best to exasperate us. However, we need to think very carefully about how we treat them and endeavour to do so clearly and fairly.

In many classroom observations I see a lack of fairness in terms of rewards and punishments. Boys frequently tend to be louder and less subtle in their lack of action or attention than girls – they are perceived to be off task, are vocal about what they don't like or see the point of, and easily incur the wrath of staff. However, many girls are regularly off task but do so in less obvious ways (texting under the table, writing notes or chatting quietly). These are often undetected or only mildly rebuked even if they are as distracting as the boys' more obvious behaviour. Similarly the reactions of teachers to missing homework, inadequate equipment or timekeeping can also be variable depending on the individual. All of these dealings are noticed by students and can lead to the feeling that a teacher is unfair or worse on the lookout to constantly punish them. It can be a great effort but it is important not to harbour feelings or expectations from previous lessons and to start afresh each day.

Similarly favouritism creates a strong negative reaction from many students. Those who conform, work hard, have a likeable personality or just know all of the answers can receive undue attention or special treatment from the teacher; it can be very hard not to show favouritism to them in the classroom. Perhaps you remember being the 'class star' at school and know how lovely it is to bask in the warmth of the teacher's attention, praise and admiration. But it is not so positive for the rest of the less 'chosen' students. Some comments from students interviewed reinforce this:

> An amazing teacher never holds a grudge. You must give a student a clean slate. This may be hard but you have to try . . .

> Teachers need to respect students as they would adults. After all we are human beings as well! If teachers have a favourite student, they shouldn't show it. Like in an army, morale needs to be kept high. Showing favour to a particular student creates bad will among others. How you teach affects the atmosphere in the classroom.

Imagine how motivating it would be if each student felt that their teacher really liked and valued them and made them feel special? Try to replicate that mood in the classroom by including, praising, rewarding and paying attention to all of your students. This is harder than it sounds because of human nature and classroom dynamics. Make sure that all students get an equal chance to join in, take lead roles and benefit from your attention. It is often the case that the most able, the least able, the best behaved, the worst behaved, the most confident (because they always ask) and the least confident (because they never do) are in the teacher's range and get sufficient attention. Be very aware of those students in the middle of the range, the seemingly unremarkable, those hitting their targets and ones that don't cause trouble. Make sure they get the time and attention they deserve too.

It is interesting that of all the possible characteristics a teacher could possess students see a sense of humour as so important. What does this mean? Does it mean that we all need an armoury of jokes, puns and wordplay ready to release upon our unsuspecting 'audience' at a moment's notice? Luckily for us, although it seems that students like a joke, what they really mean is the ability to be jovial and happy and create a less pressurised learning environment. Humour influences the classroom atmosphere, as one girl comments:

The mood of a teacher can affect their teaching ability and the lesson they are scheduled to teach. Friendly, happy and humorous teachers will perhaps build relationships with the students and give them an enjoyable lesson.

The ability to enjoy the lesson and to lighten the mood with humour can be important in creating a conducive classroom atmosphere. Learning is clearly important – it is serious stuff – but this does not mean it can't also be enjoyable and fun. If used effectively humour can also be useful to calm down potentially difficult situations: instead of getting cross, stern or angry, a funny comment can deflate or stop a student in their tracks thereby lightening the mood and avoiding conflict. An amazing teacher also knows not to take themselves too seriously and when they make a mistake can initiate the laughter rather than getting angry or feeling they have lost face.

How well do you think you rate on the criteria of teaching expertise, humour and fairness? These are areas that as well as students giving you some feedback on you can develop through a colleague observing your lesson and being aware of your own actions.

Thinking point

Teaching experience

- What questions might you ask yourself to gauge the teaching experience for your students?
- In the last week how many different activities have you tried with a class?
- When was the last time you tried a new technique?
- When did you last find a new resource or read something fresh about your subject area or attend some continuing professional development?
- What impact did this have on your lesson?

- What other questions could you ask?

Fairness

- How do you encourage students to participate and answer questions?
- In a lesson how many students join in? (Ask someone to observe and do a tally.) Do all students get involved? Is the feedback dominated by boys or girls?
- Think about one of your classes. Can you note down the names of all the students in two minutes? I'm guessing you'll remember the students at the extremes (e.g. the brightest, best behaved, naughtiest and most frustrating). If you don't recall them all make a special effort with the 'missing students' – those you found hard to recall – as these will be the ones you habitually overlook.

Humour

- If something goes wrong can you laugh about it?
- Do you have occasional 'golden moments' when the class shares a joke or laughs together?
- Do all students readily contribute to the lesson? (This is a sign of a comfortable learning environment.)
- Do you sometimes use humour and banter to diffuse conflict or get students back on track?

- Ask students to recommend a teacher who has a good sense of humour and whose classes they enjoy, then ask to observe them, ideally with a difficult class.

Chapter 3

Characteristics, Charisma and Classroom Climate

> To help students and young people learn, you need to invest time in building relationships first. You have to give respect in order to get it.
>
> Natalie Packer, SEN expert

Classroom climate can best be described by a visual image: the teacher is the captain of the ship. The seas may be rough, waves may be crashing upon the deck (think Year 8 after a wet and windy break time), the sailors may be tired, hungry or mutinous (the lesson before lunch or resistant to the test you are setting). Perhaps the ship has to cross treacherous oceans, filled with sharks and ragged rocks . . . You get the picture.

The analogy between a ship's captain and a teacher is a useful one. Captains have a huge responsibility towards their ship – they need to make important decisions and to make these with confidence and assurance. They may have a first mate (learning support assistant or other) but essentially the decisions and responsibilities are all theirs. Likewise, a captain can appear to be at the mercy of the weather. However experienced or effective he is, he cannot command the elements and at times there may be gales, storms or too much wind! Things can be turbulent for both the captain and his crew and the weather can change sometimes without a moment's notice. Sometimes it can be too still and the ship seems becalmed as students become sluggish, apathetic or lack interest. Although the teacher, like the captain, cannot always predict or forecast the mood or attitude of their students, they do retain a measure of control over it.

You may not be able to predict or regulate your class's attitude when they arrive at your lesson. They may be hot, tired or angry at what has happened in a previous lesson or what occurred at lunchtime or even before school. However, when they cross the threshold to your room they enter into 'your area' and this is something that you do control and can influence for good or otherwise. As the teacher you set and create the atmosphere in your classroom. The effect of this can be huge – setting the behaviour of more than thirty individuals for the next sixty minutes. An outstanding teacher harnesses this and sets the right atmosphere for quality learning.

What do we mean by atmosphere?

We all know what we mean when we say we like the 'atmosphere' of somewhere – perhaps a party was really lively, a restaurant has a particularly romantic feel or a shop has an exclusive, sophisticated or a trendy air. Sometimes the way this is achieved is fairly obvious: music, lighting and decoration all create a certain ambience which provokes us to act in certain ways. We can't do this in our classrooms – or can we?

Think about an occasion when the atmosphere or climate somewhere wasn't quite right, where you felt uncomfortable, awkward or anxious. Sometimes these feelings can come across very strongly but it can be difficult to put your finger on the reason why you felt so ill at ease. Much has to do with the way you are treated by others, even if on the surface things seem quite cordial. Your line manager might be saying, 'There's nothing to worry about – *but* I need a word . . .' but tiny clues can give away that actually this is far from the truth. Body language, tone of voice and even the way you use your space can all provoke a hostile or positive reaction in others. This is never more true than in the classroom.

As teachers we set and dictate the atmosphere in our classroom. It is our feelings, moods and attitudes that affect whether the lesson goes well or otherwise. What about the student and their attitudes, mood and feelings I hear you say? You would be correct in thinking that they do have an impact. However, we cannot be responsible for the attitudes and feelings of thirty others, but we can manage our own and often could do it better.

We might be secretly dreading our difficult Year 8 French bottom set during the last lesson on a Friday – but it would be disastrous to let them know that. As if you would! But you'd be surprised how often a teacher's feelings towards a class are absolutely crystal clear – not only to an outside observer but crucially to the class themselves. What do I mean? Well, perhaps an example might help.

A little while ago I was observing a newly qualified teacher (NQT). We had arranged that I would watch two classes and then feedback my observations to her. The first lesson was a delight. A Year 7 class were greeted with warmth and enthusiasm. She greeted many by name and the students waited expectantly for an exciting lesson. They received it: answers were praised, students competed to answer questions, they worked hard and some even moaned when the lesson ended. The teacher was all smiles, engaged and engaging her students by turn. I had very much enjoyed the lesson and was looking forward to feeding back some really positive comments about a very promising new teacher.

Suddenly the atmosphere chilled by several degrees as the next class bounded in. They were lively and at Year 11 much larger than the Year 7s that had just left, but what was most striking was the teacher's attitude towards them. This time there was no jovial banter at the start of the lesson, no first name terms. Standing behind her desk with arms folded she seemed poised for conflict. Students discussed their homework and started getting it out of their bags. 'No,' she snapped when they began offering their books to her. 'We have a visitor. We are starting something new.' Offended and cross they sulkily put their books away and so the lesson started.

It was a frosty, lacklustre experience on both sides. I was surprised because the good humour, enjoyment and warmth that had been so tangible with the younger students had mysteriously evaporated, leaving a humourless and irritated teacher poised to jump on any minor infringement of the rules. Students who forgot pens were berated and any whisperers were snapped at. The students 'got back at Miss' by refusing to answer her questions and by sighing loudly if asked. They grumbled and the lesson eventually ground to an end. The students left the room with some relief and the teacher looked relaxed for the first time in sixty minutes.

Packing up my notes, I made an off-the-cuff remark on what had seemed glaringly obvious to me: 'Well, you can tell you don't like them!' With that the poor NQT collapsed in a flood of tears. Unfortunately it was the truth and sadly it had been all too obvious to the students as well as to me. It was clear the teacher felt ill-equipped and lacked confidence dealing with them; moreover she clearly thought they were rude and unlikeable – and they knew it. It is not a recipe for a harmonious lesson is it?

Thinking point

- What is the weather like in your classroom?
- Think about a class or student you find challenging? What do you do to manage or improve the situation?
- Imagine you were a student in your classroom. How would you describe the climate? What are the best three things about it?
- What else could you do to improve your climate?

Classroom environment

Your classroom gives away much more than you think about *your* attitudes, *your* feelings towards *your* class and *your* passion or otherwise towards the subject you are teaching. Sometimes when the environment is effective you barely notice it, but its effect is there all the same. A purposeful, well-ordered classroom will create a purposeful and effective learning climate. When you walk into a classroom you are picking up lots of subconscious messages about the owner of the room, so looking afresh at classrooms through students' eyes can be very revealing.

Reflection moment

- In a free period visit an area of the school that you don't usually spend time in. Try to approach it with fresh eyes.
- Is it welcoming? Is it in a good state of repair? Most importantly – because sometimes we can't have the ideal buildings or beautifully painted classrooms of our dreams – does this area promote learning? Are you clear what type of lessons go on here? Do you get a strong sense of the subject? Is it clear it is a Maths/ Science/History area of learning? What can you tell about the teacher's attitude towards teaching from the environment?
- Are there exciting looking and interesting displays? Are they attractive to the eye and in a good state of repair? Do they engage and interest you? Would you be excited about learning more about cells/the Romans/algebra? If not, why not?
- Peek into some classrooms. How are they set out? Can everybody see the board? Does it look well organised and cared for?
- What is on the walls? Is the room attractive as a learning environment? Would it be a safe and interesting place to learn? Are key words related to the topic displayed to reinforce literacy skills?
- What encourages you to get involved? Are there interesting and interactive displays? Research books or tools? Would you want to get involved?

Note down three things that you have seen that impressed you or had a positive influence in the classrooms you have visited. Think about whether any of these things could be successfully adapted in your classroom. Don't be shy about asking your colleagues for tips or asking where they found their resources. Everybody likes a bit of praise and if they have spent effort in creating an effective learning environment and it shows, tell them! It is likely they will happily give you some advice that you could use in your own classroom.

- Think about one negative aspect that you have seen? What could be done to improve it?

- Now go back to your own area and have a look through fresh eyes. Try sitting in some of the students' seats. What do they see? Is there anything you could do to make your classroom into a more charismatic and attractive learning environment for both you and your students?

Thinking point

Your own environment can be used to your advantage. It can help with classroom management, getting students interested and engaged and telling them lots of important information about you before you've even spoken a word. You don't believe me? Well read on.

In a school year I see hundreds of different classrooms and hundreds of different teachers. Sometimes I might be visiting a school with which I am very familiar but more often than not I am walking into a new classroom for the first time. What I see and what your students see is very revealing. It is always possible to tell whether a teacher has genuine enthusiasm for their subject, how well organised they are and whether they value and are interested in their students. The classroom walls are a key indicator about how the teacher sees their subject and their level of interest in it.

Colourful, vibrant displays that include pictures, photographs, text and of course students' work can make even the dreariest classroom into an enticing and interesting area. As a student you often sit in the same seat, gazing at the same section of wall. An interesting and lively display creates a purposeful learning environment and on a subliminal level makes various, key statements about the teacher's attitude to the subject and student expectations. The following are examples of good practice I have seen, but keep alert and you will have many more to add to your repertoire.

- Laminate a large notice with your name on it. Put this on a noticeboard at the front of the classroom. It will avoid the misspelling of your name on your exercise books and will help to establish the classroom as your own area.

- Ask your head of department for some backing paper and think about the colour you choose. Black is serious but bright colours can really liven up a classroom wall.

- Think about creating some work with your classes in the early weeks which can be used as a display. It needs to be meaningful work with a real purpose, but getting classes to show off their own work early on will give them a sense of ownership and pride. It will also make you look cool and relaxed come the September round of open evenings for prospective parents – when everyone else is clamouring for work to display.

- Always create a small sign explaining which year group's work it is and some detail about the task so that parents and other students understand the context of the work. If you laminate these you can add them to your resources for next year.

- Backing students' work onto card or other coloured paper will always make it look smarter, but it can be time consuming. Encourage keen students to help with putting up displays (under your supervision) or speak to your head of department about administrative support to help.

- Even in redrafted work, students will make errors, so correct these in pencil. It shows you have looked at the work and means you are not reinforcing errors.

- If you have plenty of noticeboards in your classroom think about designating one for each of your classes. This will ensure you have a balance of work on display (not just Year 7 and 8 students) and can create a real sense of belonging and motivation. For example: 'Your character charts and collages will be used in your talks, but they are also going to be put on display, so I'm also offering merits for those that are eye-catching!'

- Effective displays aren't just pretty wallpaper – they should be so much more. When you start a new topic with students think about ways of introducing it visually. Laminating key words is a good way of emphasising key vocabulary and spelling. Mind maps, text extracts and colourful displays which really entice students to read the information are a good way of reinforcing learning or introducing key topics. Perhaps at the start of the year, if you are teaching story writing to Year 8, for example, some interesting opening lines from a range of different novels could be placed on large sheets of coloured paper or perhaps some intriguing pictures to provoke their creative spark? Headings which ask questions or even suggest a competition are also a good way of getting students involved.

- Pictures, posters and diagrams are also good for reinforcing key learning objectives. This was used to good effect in a lesson I observed recently: a Year 10 boy asked his teacher for permission to look at another group's wall chart because he remembered they had used a key fact that he wanted to include in his essay. This shows how displays can really benefit the learning of students in the classroom.

- Check displays and refresh them at least each half term. A sharp eye and a ready staple gun can repair the inevitable tears that even the best mounted work will suffer. If the display looks tired or dated then it is well worth putting in the effort to renew it.

- Be creative! Don't be shy of asking bookshops, travel agents and other businesses for old posters. One travel agent told me he found it such a shame to be throwing out beautiful high quality posters of exotic travel locations – these could be used in Geography classes or as stimulus for writing in English lessons. If you explain that you are a teacher staff are usually thrilled to give you last season's displays which, with a little ingenuity, can be used as an excellent teaching resource and enticing display: all for free!

Managing behaviour through the learning environment

Can the way you use your classroom really help with managing students' behaviour? Certainly. The way you act in the classroom and the way it is set out can make or break your classroom management. If it is organised, clean and tidy this sends out the signal that you expect students to look after and respect the room. Make an effort to ensure that students clean up any paper or rubbish at the end of the lesson and that they straighten desks and chairs. It makes a clear statement that your environment matters and that you are in control of it. You may be wondering why the classroom environment matters – surely it is *what* I am teaching them that matters most? In a sense you are right; a carefully constructed learning environment does not automatically mean that effective learning will go on, but it is a good start.

Thinking point

Consider the following and think about whether the way you use your classroom could help with managing student behaviour.

One day as an adviser I had been asked to observe a particular teacher and give them some feedback on their lessons. Walking into the classroom I observed a pyramid of broken chairs in one corner, paper strewn across the floor, books stuffed down radiators and masses of unadorned, yawning grey display boards. Just entering the room depressed me and it was little surprise that the students appeared to be disaffected and poorly behaved. The lesson itself was entirely unsuccessful. It was chaotic and badly planned, some activities went on for far too long and some instructions were given so quickly it was difficult to know what the students had to do next. However I had some sympathy for the teacher. She was clearly travelling from room to room and was expected to put up with an undermining and hopelessly messy environment. How, I wondered, could she possibly hope to instil a positive working atmosphere and impress her authority on the class when her students were made to work in such an unpleasant space?

Imagine my surprise when I commiserated with her about her lack of a permanent classroom to be told that, 'Actually I do have one: this is it!' It would have only taken a few hours and a little motivation to make the war zone look like a pleasant and welcoming space, but her failure to take responsibility for it and to make even the smallest effort spoke volumes about her attitude towards teaching and her students. Judging by her students' behaviour I wasn't the only one to pick up on it.

So what can you do? Assert your authority by:

- Deciding how you want the desks set out and arranging them.
- Make sure that everyone can see the board properly.
- It is your classroom: you decide on the seating plan. Make a paper copy.
- Be hot on graffiti. Some desks may be marked. Ask the caretaker nicely if it can be removed. Check desks after each lesson and be known for zero tolerance.
- Get broken chairs and equipment fixed promptly.
- Model showing respect to books and equipment and expect students to do the same.
- Talk about the classroom as 'our' room and encourage students to take roles such as book monitor, date writer, plant monitor, etc.
- Make it a pleasant environment using colourful and informative displays.

- Make your classroom rules clear: ensure students know that they need to ask permission to move out of their seats. You decide on whether the windows are opened or closed, not them.

- Use the classroom display boards to show your passion for the subject and to publicly celebrate the latest efforts of your classes.

But what if you don't have your own classroom and are forced into teaching across different areas of the school? Make the best of this by:

- Finding out who else you share the room with. Perhaps it is one other teacher, in which case if you are tactful you might be able to negotiate taking over the responsibility for a particular display board. Most of us would be glad to have someone who wants to help.

- Ask if there is somewhere you can store some of your resources.

- Be flexible. This might mean seating your students in a layout that is not to your preference, but see this as a way of trying out a new system.

- The classroom may not be arranged the same, but still insist that students sit in the order and way you want them to.

- Learn from other areas of the school. Pinch good ideas for displays and teaching ideas from the other areas you visit.

- Be well organised. If you are a ten-minute trip from the Geography block then running out of paper or pens is not a good idea. Ask if you can store some nearby or keep a small supply with you.

- Remember, even if you don't have your own classroom, by adopting the same routines and rituals at the start of each lesson you will help to settle your students and put yourself firmly in charge.

Reflection moment

Have a look at your classroom with a fresh pair of eyes. Think about how you can persuade students that learning your subject is an interesting and worthwhile experience; how will your environment and attitude will reinforce this?

Three simple changes I am going to make to my classroom environment or my attitude towards my students in the next fortnight are:

1.

2.

3.

I will review these on ____________.

What went well?

What could have been better?

Chapter 4

Teaching Outstanding Lessons and Learning from Other Teachers

> Outstanding lessons require outstanding planning with a relentless focus on maximising learning so that it is at least very good. The extra bit is the true sense of enjoyment that everyone has in a collaborative learning environment that allows students to take a real lead in their learning.
>
> Jamie Clarke, head teacher of Sponne School, Technology College and Ofsted inspector

One of the things teachers and students are in agreement about is that an amazing teacher really can teach! Their lessons are inspiring or as Ofsted calls them 'outstanding'. However before we can hope to aspire to these dizzying heights of excellence we need to be clear on this very nebulous term. Then of course we need to think about how this translates into what we actually do in the classroom.

We all want our lessons to be good – really good. This is not because of Ofsted (although it is certainly affirming to be told that your lesson is outstanding, even if a little voice tells you that if she'd seen your Year 9 last thing on a Friday you'd be lucky to get satisfactory) but because you want the students in your classes to have a good experience, enjoy your lessons and importantly make progress and achieve because of your teaching.

But what does Ofsted mean by outstanding and are there any characteristics you should be looking to include in your lessons? If I wanted to bake a fantastic cake, I could look up a recipe, buy all the listed ingredients, carefully measure them out, combine them all, follow the instructions and hey presto what I ended up with would look something pretty close to the picture.

Teaching isn't quite like this and thank goodness, because imagine how dull it would be! You cannot hope to exactly follow somebody else's lesson plan to provide an outstanding lesson. What might have worked brilliantly with your colleague's Year 10 class may be completely unsuitable for your own group and their needs. Their outstanding lesson formula may flounder if it is churned out in an unassimilated way by somebody else.

So does this mean that an outstanding lesson has a certain mystical quality that we cannot expect to replicate? Certainly not. There are plenty of ways to ensure that your lessons are the best they can possibly be. It is always worth looking at the Ofsted criteria for lesson judgements which can be found on the their website (www.ofsted.gov.uk) and there are practical things to consider in the planning and delivering of your own lessons to ensure that you teach to your best. The current definition of outstanding presupposes that many of the aspects of good teaching will feature in the lesson. One of the key phrases in the description is that the teaching leads to the 'result that the students are making *exceptional* progress. [Teaching] is highly effective in inspiring students and ensuring that they learn extremely well.' The word 'progress' here is significant and when you are planning lessons it is important to keep this at the forefront of your mind.

But what exactly does progress mean and why is it such a crucial indicator of an outstanding lesson? In all lessons you want students to *enjoy* the learning experience, but what will really mark out the lesson as being an exceptional learning experience is the amount of *progress* the students make. This point is important; even in a short period of time progress should be made. How has their learning moved on? What do they know now that they didn't before? How has the experience of being in the lesson deepened their knowledge and understanding?

Lesson planning for amazing lessons

The deepening of knowledge and understanding should be the key factors when planning lessons. Don't think about what *tasks* students will be doing, instead concentrate on the *learning*. What skills do you want them to master? What can they do already and therefore what should be their next learning steps? For example, perhaps you are teaching your class *Macbeth* for a piece of coursework. They know the storyline pretty well and are beginning to select appropriate quotations from the text. What exactly do they need to get them to the next level? In this case they need to learn how to start commenting on their quotations and then learning how to analyse the language. The lesson and the tasks should ensure that these objectives are met.

Just because students are cooperative and working well don't always assume that your lesson will be classed automatically as outstanding. Students can become immersed in activities that are simply good fun but that may not move on their learning sufficiently well for progress to be good enough. You will obviously get a feel for how well your lesson is going, but it is always worth considering how much the students are learning and progressing as well as of course enjoying themselves.

Difficult classroom behaviour

Of course we want our students to be engaged and excited but sometimes the fact that students are on task and enjoying themselves can fool us into thinking that our lessons are better than they actually are. Obviously poor classroom behaviour inhibits good learning and it is impossible to concentrate, for student and teacher alike, if there is a riot ensuing. However don't presume that you can't teach an outstanding lesson to a difficult class or that the occasional behaviour problem will mean that your lesson is judged as inadequate. It is how the behaviour is dealt with that is important.

One of my colleagues was inspected with a lively Year 9 class. Her lesson was going well and all students were participating enthusiastically when suddenly a couple at the front loudly proclaimed, 'This is rubbish, we're not doing any more.' They threw down their pens and rested their head on their hands. Midway through an explanation of a task, the teacher was horrified and looked across at the inspector who was busily making notes. Feeling that she had blown the observation, she just decided to do what she would normally do: deal with the behaviour appropriately but keep focused on the lesson. She acknowledged the students' comments with a firm remark but refused to get sidetracked. Then, while the rest of the class were working hard on the task, she remonstrated with the students who were still being sullen and uncooperative, eventually separating them. One sullenly got on with their work and one did not and was removed by a senior member of staff and later given a detention.

In the plenary the class demonstrated an assured knowledge about the topic and through sharing their responses showed to what extent their learning had progressed. The teacher, heart in her mouth, waited to see what the inspector would say about the miscreants but was surprised to receive a glowing comment about the lesson, focusing on the progress the students had made as a class. When she observed that she had expected to be penalised for the two students' poor behaviour she was relieved to hear that the inspector thought she had dealt with them effectively and had stopped their misbehaviour from impeding the learning of the class as a whole.

This echoes a comment made by a student interviewed about the skills needed by an amazing teacher. Acknowledging that sometimes other students' behaviour can get out of hand, this Year 9 boy said, 'If you get a troublesome kid they must be dealt with: for example, if you have a student who is refusing to work or sit down, etc. give them choices, e.g. they either sit down or leave the room . . . When students misbehave, they can disturb the learning of others, so something *must* be done about it.'

There's plenty that can be said about outstanding lessons and how to achieve them, but have a look at the following ten questions. These are some of the ingredients that make for a really good lesson. They are worth bearing in mind when you are planning your lessons, but don't agonise too much about each one. Perhaps see which ones you think are your strengths and which one would make a good focus for your next term's targets. Everybody's lessons vary across the week and even lesson to lesson – even Advanced Skills Teachers. As individuals we have days when we think that we are a pretty good teacher and other days when we wonder about our abilities. But one of the best things about teaching is that, like our students, we should always be keen to learn and improve.

Thinking point

Key questions to think about when planning your outstanding lessons:

1. How have I planned this lesson so that all students progress?

2. How does it fit with their prior learning?

3. How will I know in the lesson that students have achieved? What will I build into my plenary to demonstrate this?

4. If I realise learning is insecure or students make a great point or connection, am I flexible enough to adapt my lesson?

5. How do I manage behaviour in lessons so that it is good and does not distract from learning? Have I got a positive learning atmosphere in the lessons?

6. Is my knowledge of the subject matter confident and accurate and used to good effect?

7. Have I planned to use a range of engaging teaching techniques so that students are interested and motivated and learn well?

8. Are my books well marked and do I know the learning needs of my students?

9. If I have teaching assistants or other staff in my lessons do I work well with them so that they add to the students' progress?

10. Are students aware of their next steps in learning and do I use (when appropriate) strategies for getting them to self-assess their work?

Learning from other teachers – the amazing, the adequate and those that fall in between

> Use your colleagues; in a good way. They will all have huge stores of completely different knowledge and resources. Learn from them and share with them.
>
> Ian Kirby, acting head of department and teacher, Roade School, Sports College

It can be hard to look critically at your own performance and this is where having a friendly observer can be useful. I stress the idea of 'friendly' observations because some school evaluations often provide only a snapshot of a lesson and reviewers have very little time to provide feedback or discuss the finer points of your lesson – and this is what is really needed if you are to improve.

One way of pinpointing some of the skills of the amazing teacher is to see a skilled colleague at work. Very often it is common knowledge who are the most engaging and effective teachers. Senior leadership teams should have an awareness of the teaching strengths and experience of different staff members and even if you are new to a school you should be able to ask for guidance about who would be good to observe. I firmly believe though that you can learn something from every lesson, particularly if you go in with an open mind and have time to discuss what you have seen with the teacher you have observed.

Think about what it is that you wish to learn from the experience. If you are keen to learn more engaging and interesting strategies for teaching your subject area then it obviously makes sense to watch a colleague who teaches a similar subject or who has classes of a similar ability. Don't just limit your ideas to observing in your own school. Often within an institution ideas are already fruitfully exchanged between staff members. A visit to a good department in a different local school might yield all kinds of imaginative ideas. They may have entirely different resources, imaginative ways of structuring the curriculum or be experts with technology that your school has yet to hear of . . .

School leaders may not be very keen on you nipping out of your lessons to observe others, but it is worthwhile and useful professional development. However, to make the most of it, do your homework. You can learn a great deal about how *not* to do it in a bad lesson, and it can be falsely reassuring to go back to your own class content that all is well in your world – by comparison!

It is advisable to search out a really outstanding department. Word of mouth, Ofsted reports, examination results and recommendations of local or national advisers might all be worth considering as a starting point.

Make sure with any observation you undertake to get some information about the class and their ability beforehand. You would obviously expect to see a different lesson with students aiming for an A* grade compared to those trying to achieve a grade E. Information like this is important for establishing whether what is expected of the class is challenging enough for them. Also ensure that the teacher you are observing has some time to talk to you, even if it is just discussing your ideas over a sandwich at lunchtime.

If you are more interested in refining your classroom management skills, stretching students of different abilities or managing challenging classes then consider watching one of your own classes when they are being taught by someone in a different subject specialism. Sometimes distancing the actual teaching skills from the subject knowledge can be really useful.

Just because you are a Maths teacher and you choose to watch a History lesson doesn't necessarily mean that teaching strategies aren't transferable. Different subject areas often have valuable ways of managing group work, teaching key concepts or involving students in their own learning that can be effectively transferred.

When watching the lesson have a look at the key questions for planning an outstanding lesson (see page 60), but as the lesson progresses try to raise your head above your notepad and reflect upon what you are experiencing.

Thinking point

- How does it feel to be in *this* classroom?
- What does it look like? Is it a pleasant learning environment? Can all the students see the board?
- How do I feel? What is the learning climate like? If I was a student would I be feeling interested? Engaged? Bored? Frightened? Intimidated? Challenged? Interested?

- What is the atmosphere like in the classroom and how has that been created? Do students feel they can answer questions? How do other students respond?

- How does the teacher react towards the students? Are they friendly? Encouraging? Do they push and challenge them enough?

- What are the students doing? Are they actively engaged? What is the pace of the lesson like?

Make sure you walk around the classroom and engage with the students. In an amazing lesson students will be able to tell you what they are learning and list the learning objectives. They will happily discuss and show you their work and they will take some obvious enjoyment from this.

Try to learn from any good practice you notice. Does the teacher have a particular way of organising groups, gaining students' attention or moving on the lesson that works well? Equally important is how the teacher manages things that go awry. How do they get a student back on task, clarify poor instructions or diffuse a potentially hostile interaction? A skilled teacher's lessons don't always go to plan, but what is interesting is how they manage any issues and resolve problems – even if these were of their own making. Even amazing teachers aren't perfect, but their success lies in their ability to know when things aren't going well and changing or adapting their lesson plan as necessary.

Keep a record of what you have noticed working well. Are there any ideas, tips or strategies that you could borrow, adapt or make your own? Be aware that a technique may seem to serve one teacher very well, but like a poorly fitting suit may swamp or be totally unsuitable when you try it on. But try them you must . . .

Think about any mysteries or things you are unclear about in what you have seen. Why is it that one girl sits on her own with her back to the rest of the class? What did the teacher say very quietly to the angry boy that stopped him kicking off? How does the reward and homework policy work? You get the picture. Be aware that the lesson might not have gone directly as the teacher planned and they may have made alterations when they realised they'd forgotten an important handout or noticed that something wasn't working as well as it might. These are all good teaching skills to learn.

Finally, it is important to thank and acknowledge the teacher for being brave enough to invite you into their lesson. When being an observer we can sometimes forget just how nerve-wracking it is having another person in the lesson. Bear in mind that even your presence, however friendly and unobtrusive you have tried to be, will have influenced and thereby changed the classroom environment and dynamic. Before you ask your myriad of questions, make sure you mention some things about the lesson that impressed or interested you. And offer to return the favour – because being observed by somebody with insight is one way of gaining really helpful feedback to let you know what is working and what the next steps should be on your journey to developing amazing teaching skills.

Reflection moment

Have a look at the following pro forma. The idea is that by 'dipping' into lessons you can get a feel for what is going on and how students are learning across a range of subjects. It is a way of focusing on a particular aspect of learning. This can be a very useful tool for a senior manager trying to get a handle on the quality of teaching across their school.

However, if you are observing on your own just pick a couple of the areas to focus on.

In developing the skills of an amazing teacher it is also important to think about how you can work on each of these areas yourself. Try to watch a range of lessons to see how skilful teachers manage each of these areas to see what tips you can glean from them. Perhaps when you are having your lessons observed you can suggest the observer looks at a particular area. You will also notice that the pro forma addresses what the *students* are doing, and most importantly *learning*, which is after all the criteria for teaching the most successful and amazing lessons.

Lesson focus pro forma for lesson 'dipping'

The purpose of this exercise is to get an understanding of the current situation regarding aspects of Assessment for Learning in a range of lessons. The focus of the observation is on the students and what they are doing, how they are working and what they know. Dipping into a range of lessons at different times will give some indication of the current state of Assessment for Learning in the school. The following feedback sheet will be completed as appropriate.

Focus	Notes
Students experience a range of interactive and appropriate teaching approaches.	
Students are aware of what they are learning. Lesson objectives are used as appropriate.	
Students know from feedback where they are and what they need to do next to make improvements.	
Students receive regular feedback (oral or written).	
A good range of students are involved in questions. Questioning helps improve students' understanding. There is a suitable level of challenge.	

Building strategies that turn an acceptable classroom into an amazing classroom

This section looks at the finer details of what we need to do to make our teaching amazing. Firstly we need to reflect upon what it is like to be a student in our lessons. We need to think about not only what they are achieving but how the students in our charge feel. As mentioned previously, how students feel and how we create a positive climate for learning is vital for good learning.

Secondly it can be useful to reflect upon the types of behaviour we are exhibiting as the teacher and what this tells us about the types of values we have in our classroom. Before you go any further make sure you have at least fifteen minutes uninterrupted quiet to focus on the following task. (I know in a busy school it can be difficult to get just five minutes, but you really need this period of time to get the best out of the next task. If you don't have it now, then skip to the next chapter. Don't read on any further . . . you'll spoil it for yourself if you do!)

Right, take a look at the characteristics below. Read through them and then think about the following. I am going to ask you to write on this sheet, but you will want to take a copy of it first.

Self-reflection exercise

Consider each of these characteristics:

encouraging
enthusiastic
brave
loyal
caring
generous
diligent
serious
supportive
happy
anxious
positive
inspiring
considerate
determined
helpful
thoughtful
ambitious
conservative
practical
hardworking
intelligent
creative
enterprising
sympathetic
analytical
organised
thoughtful
careful
energetic
humorous
tolerant
adventurous
focused
flexible
ordered
organised
forward thinking
gregarious
impatient
patient
artistic
sincere
purposeful
assertive
persuasive
calm
lively
cheerful
approachable
tactful
good tempered
fair
modest
adventurous
trusting
direct
confident
resourceful

Which five characteristics do you think you most possess? Use your own estimation of your qualities, paying attention to those you think you have, not those you *wish* you possessed. Circle in pencil the five that you think are most representative of you.

Look at the list again and circle (in a different colour) two further adjectives describing qualities you believe you do not possess.

Thinking point

Step 1

Take a moment's reflection on the activity. Did you enjoy doing it? If you didn't or felt it was an uncomfortable experience, why was this? Did it make you think about your behaviour – perhaps reflecting on our own skills is a difficult task? If you did not enjoy it, did you complete it? Did you think about leaving it out? Use this experience of having to do something that you would rather not do to remind you of what it is like being a student and being forced to complete arduous exercises or tasks where the point of the activity is not always very clear at the start. Look again at the characteristics you have selected. What evidence do you have that you are calm / patient / enthusiastic? Can you think of a moment from the last week where you exhibited these qualities?

Step 2

What do you think your students or other teachers would say about your key characteristics? Do you think they would select the same ones as you? Are you interested in finding out? The idea of this task is not only to make you reflect upon what sorts of characteristics you have – but also to think about how you are perceived by your students and others. After all it is not very useful, if you think you are a calm and encouraging teacher, if the students' perception is that you have a very short fuse and insist that *you* are always right! (I am sure that this is not the case – however we can all think of people from our everyday life whose self-views are in complete contrast to the reality of how they are perceived.)

Step 3

I am not necessarily suggesting that you distribute this sheet to all of your classes. For a start many of them won't have the maturity to deal with it but with some groups, such as sixth formers, it might lead to an interesting discussion. It can also be used to thought-provoking effect with family, friends and colleagues. But even if you don't actually do anything else with it, use it to help you reflect.

Look again at the characteristics and consider them with an eye to you as an amazing teacher. Which five characteristics do you most want to exhibit and what actions or behaviours do you need to demonstrate to make them possible for you? Be brave! Take up a pen, make a note of them and incorporate them into your everyday behaviours.

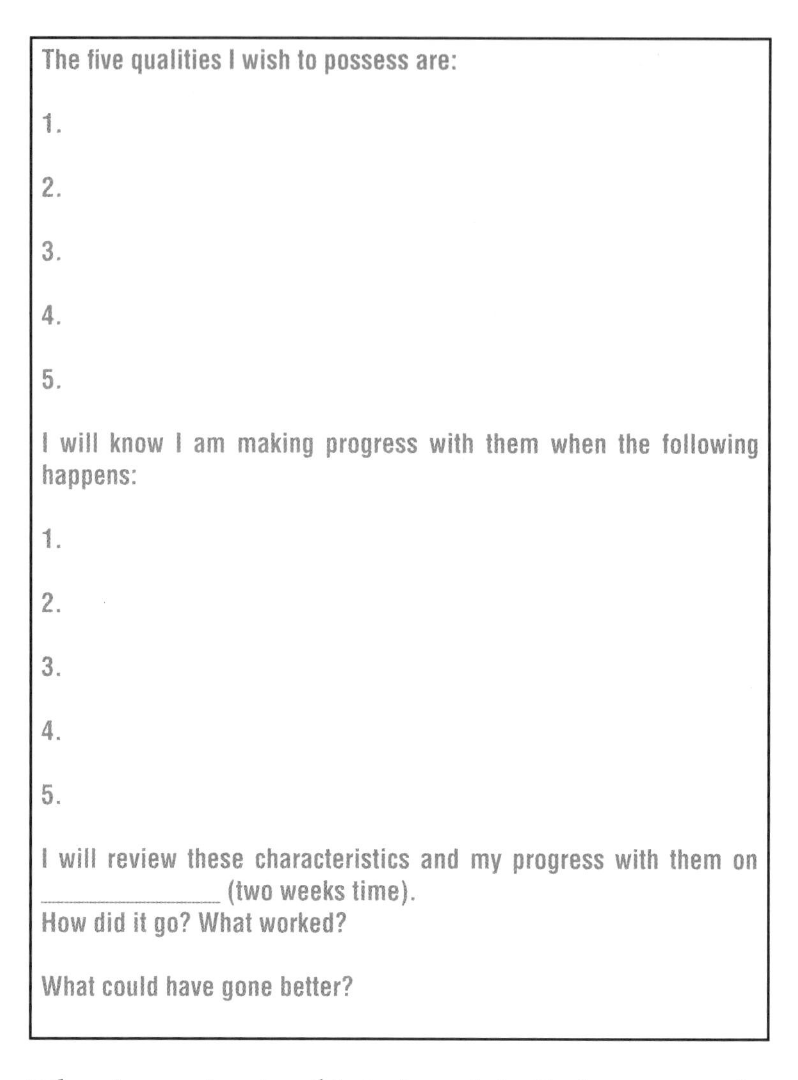

The five qualities I wish to possess are:

1.

2.

3.

4.

5.

I will know I am making progress with them when the following happens:

1.

2.

3.

4.

5.

I will review these characteristics and my progress with them on ________________ (two weeks time).
How did it go? What worked?

What could have gone better?

When I was planning this task – originally for a course for middle managers – I decided I should give it a go (after all we should never make our students undertake something that we are not willing to do ourselves!). After duly ringing the characteristics I felt I possessed, I sent copies to a whole range of people.

I sent them in envelopes that I had addressed so that they would be anonymous and confidently waited for confirmation of what I thought I knew. I had sent them to head teachers in schools where I had helped to make good progress, head teachers who thought I was argumentative because we had disagreed on issues, newly qualified teachers who had been on my training sessions and members of a team I had managed.

I was astounded by the results. When I opened up the first few I compared their responses to my own: they had got it wrong – not one of them had ringed the right words. After I read a few more I was surprised to find some consistency in the responses. When I discussed these 'erroneous' findings with my husband – and prepared to dismiss them – he made a very good point: 'If one person calls you a horse, ignore them – but if six do, buy yourself a saddle!' Although none of the comments were negative (take a careful look at the questionnaire – it does not encourage this response), it did highlight that I was perceived to have some qualities that I did not realise I had (a bonus!) but also that some of the skills I thought were really obvious and crucial in my day-to-day dealings with others did not emerge. This led to some interesting thoughts: if these qualities were still my key qualities maybe I needed to reflect them a little more strongly through my behaviour and actions, as well as my words.

Chapter 5

Lesson Planning

> It is good common sense to tell your students what they will be learning that lesson.
>
> Kate Lewis, Advanced Skills Teacher,
> Arthur School, Peterborough ”

One of the most crucial aspects in planning a good lesson is the effectiveness of lesson objectives. A good lesson needs to make it absolutely clear right at the start, midway through and certainly by the end of the lesson what it is that the students have been *learning*. It is essential that the skills they are learning are made explicit and that the lesson is geared around this. All too often instructions and guidance to students focuses far too much on the task rather than the skills.

Sometimes in a lesson you might write the *learning objective* or *learning intention* (these are just different terms for the same thing) on the board. Students write these down and hopefully it is clear to them what they should be learning. However if every lesson started like this it would be terribly boring for students because although it offers a structured start, it doesn't exactly excite or grab the attention of the class or lead to speculation. Perhaps you intend to discuss or start a new topic, so it might be more intriguing and a much better opening to a lesson to display a picture to get students speculating or even start with a mystery object – the ideas are endless.

All of this excitement would be destroyed if students dutifully copied out the objective, as it might give away that the picture they are looking at is about an earthquake or that *Macbeth* is about power and kingship. There's nothing wrong in making them think and using an engaging activity to start this thinking process. However it is important that at some point during the lesson the learning objective is made clear and the learning is discussed with the students; if this is not done then the links between learning can be lost.

It is also very important that in planning you give enough thought to what the students should be *learning* as well as *doing*. This sounds fairly obvious but all too often lesson planning can focus on tasks rather than the learning objective, with disastrous results. Students become focused on the task they have completed, rather than the skills they have learnt.

We need to think carefully about what it is we want the students to learn and then consider the most appropriate task to help them fulfil this.

Before we plan any of our exciting lessons we need to stop and remind ourselves what it is that we expect our students to learn. We need to make sure that the activity supports this objective and that the learning is clear to the students.

Thinking point

You may need to think about how you make the learning obvious in your lessons. It can be a good idea to ask someone to watch your lessons to see whether they can work out what it is the students are learning. This is particularly effective if it is a colleague who teaches in a different subject area because if you are clear about your learning objectives it should be apparent to someone who is not a subject specialist.

Make good use of the students in your lesson. Ask them at the end of the lesson what it is they think they have *learnt* as well as what they have done.

Remember, it is fine to set students *tasks* – that is how you test whether they have mastered their skills and to what degree. However build in *success criteria* that relate to the actual skills, so that students are very clear about what it is they should be learning.

Have a look at the following self-check list. Remember, sometimes you can think you do something but this might not always be the case or it might not be as successful as you think it is. Why not buddy up with a colleague and agree to watch each other's lessons as part of a supportive pair?

Do you use lesson objectives effectively?	Reflects your current practice	Is partially in place	Is an area to check/ develop
Your own lesson planning uses clear, precise lesson objectives. You start your planning from the position of what the students need to *learn* next.			
Lesson objectives are shared with students when appropriate. Sometimes students speculate about what the *objective* is or should be. This discussion helps the learning.			
Lesson objectives are placed into student-friendly language wherever possible.			
Where objectives are not made explicit at the start of the lesson, somewhere in the lesson the *learning* is reviewed and the intentions are made clear.			

If they are asked during a lesson, students can usually tell you what they are learning or what they need to do to make their work successful.			
Students are told the bigger picture about how that individual lesson's objectives fits into the long-term plan (i.e. the GCSE specification).			
When appropriate, an objective is clarified by *success criteria*. This indicates what students need to show they can do to be successful.			
Questioning and explaining by the teacher is largely focused on the objective.			
If somebody else was watching the lesson it would be clear what the students were learning, not just doing.			

Starting Your Lessons in the Right Way

Structure is important! Have the same structure to each lesson; students like to have routine: get students to write the date and learning objective, then proceed to starter activity and main part of lesson and end with a plenary.

Rebecca Garvin-Elliot, head of department, Roade School Sports College

The way you start your lesson is vitally important. We have already looked at some aspects behind promoting a positive classroom environment and how this can affect students' learning. Well, what about when you have got them all looking attentive and interested? What you do in the first few crucial minutes really matters.

Prawn cocktail or pate, Sir? If the word 'starter' conjures up the impression of something delicious to get you started then you are quite right. The restaurant term has been borrowed for classroom use and relates to the fact that a fast opening starter sets the lesson off on the right track and whets the students' appetite for the main course or rest of the lesson.

The evidence of observing hours of lessons shows that the first few minutes are key. Students are restless by nature, so any teacher who demonstrates they have a clear purpose and expects active student participation in the first five minutes is more likely to grab their students' attention and get the lesson off to a flying start.

The key to getting students engaged and motivated is to get them in the right frame of mind: focused and ready to learn. The next time you observe a lesson or plan one yourself make a special point of considering how the teacher engages the students right from the moment they enter the classroom. Is there an interactive start, thinking activity, puzzle or other focus at the start of the lesson? Do students make the transition between the previous lesson smoothly so that learning takes places soon after the students enter the classroom or is there 'dead' time while the teacher waits for the rest of the class, chases homework or chastises latecomers?

Having a quick starter activity that lasts between five and fifteen minutes means that students become absorbed in the new lesson. Conversations about last night's TV, the horrors of Maths or what happened at lunchtime become difficult if students are given an interesting, short activity they know they have only a short time to complete.

So what makes a good starter? Bear in mind the following pointers:

- **Relate the starter to the learning objective of the lesson.** For example, perhaps you are going to teach a Year 7 class how to write a good story opening. An interesting starter might be to give students eight or so different story openings on cards and ask them to rank them in order of preference and explain their reasoning. Maybe you have been discussing a science experiment: getting students to logically order the steps in the experiment will engage and get them interested.

- **Consider a brief recap to secure a learning point from the previous lesson.** For example, perhaps your Year 10 French class has been writing formal letters and the interactive whiteboard – showing a letter with mistakes or missing words – could be shown and the class have five minutes to discuss in pairs what the omissions are and to correct them. Make it clear how this relates to the rest of the lesson and how it fits in with what has gone before.

- **Get visual!** If you have yet to come across a visualiser then you really need to get your hands on one for your classroom. These ingenious devices are simple to use. They look like an old fashioned overhead projector, yet once switched on they display whatever you choose onto your screen or whiteboard. The opportunities for creating a good starter are obvious. Instead of photocopying or scanning a piece of students' work, the text or artwork can be placed under the visualiser and immediately displayed, even if it is in a thick exercise book. You could also display postcards, photographs, objects, plants or magazine articles – the opportunities for capturing students' attention and using it to kick off a great learning activity are endless. Best of all you don't need any other specialised equipment and being portable buying at least one visualiser for the department is a shrewd investment – except of course everyone will want one once they see how useful they are in lessons – and not just for starters.

- **Get the students thinking. Give them the opportunity to discuss their answer with a partner.** If there is the opportunity to do this students often give more thoughtful answers as they are able to rehearse them with their partner and there is less likelihood of them saying 'can't/won't do it' too readily.

- **Make sure you give clear instructions.** The best starters are usually simple. If the activity takes fifteen minutes to explain then it is likely that some students will switch off before you have finished or become frustrated because they will have misunderstood it. Keep it clear and straightforward. Perhaps even write the instructions on the board to reinforce them. This is also helpful for managing straggling latecomers. For example:

'Think of five questions you would like to ask about this line: "And watched her thrashed for almost drowning".' Intrigued? Students often are. Giving students crystal-clear instructions means that they are confident about what they need to do and can get going as you hand out paper or take the register.

- **Give a set time limit and expect full participation.** Students won't hurry to start if they think they have got forever or that somebody else will answer for them. Start assertively by saying: 'You have five minutes in pairs to rank order these essay introductions. Decide which is the best, then the second best and be prepared to defend your choice. I will be choosing six pairs at random to feedback, so you all need to have decided on your choice.'

- **If the starter reveals that the students have not grasped a concept be prepared to adapt your lesson plan to remedy this.** If your starter was a way of getting the students to recap the main characteristics of earthquakes which you were planning to develop in the main body of the lesson, yet your starter reveals that a large number of the students have not grasped the basics then it will be necessary to teach this again. You will need to find another way of explaining it or use different examples so that the students are secure in their learning.

- **A good starter is one that gets students to think and become involved in their learning.** Good starters can involve card sort activities, highlighting texts, picking out key words or answering questions on mini-whiteboards and showing these to the class. The more involved students are with what they are doing the more likely they are to learn and think carefully about their response to the task.

Teaching strategies. How many of these techniques do you use with your students?	Rarely	Sometimes	Often	Unknown
Get students to work in pairs to discuss before answering questions				
Use concept or mind mapping				
Model yourself how to write/do the piece of work				
Use students' work to demonstrate something and teach them to critique it				
Ask them to 'go for five' when starting a topic				
Use cloze procedure (p. 89)				
Use diamond ranking/diamond nine (p. 86)				
Ask students to discuss and trial out various strategies for learning and feedback to the class				
Give groups responsibility for different tasks/questions and expect them to feedback				
Ask students to think of the appropriate success criteria for the work				
Ask students to rank order, prioritise or classify information				
Use highlighters for active reading strategies				
Use mini-whiteboards for immediate feedback to questions				

Students give PowerPoint presentations, videos, etc. on key learning				
Ask students to devise mnemonics to help with key learning				
Ask students to reduce information into five words or sentences				
Get students to devise appropriate quizzes on topics				
Use response partners to comment on each other's work and peer-assess				
Use drama skills such as role play, hot seat, improvisation, freeze frames, etc.				
Create maps from memory: working in a group students are given a time-limited observation				
Ask students to generate their own questions				
Give students answers and expect them to decide on what the question was (review of topic/plenary)				
Use a visual/auditory stimulus at the beginning of the lesson to pique students' interest				
Please add any additional techniques that you regularly use				

Five ideas for interesting and engaging starter activities

1. Diamond ranking

This activity centres around prioritisation. It can be used in many subjects and lessons where there is a benefit in students rank ordering ideas. The theory is that you give students a number of reasons or ideas. For example, I have seen it successfully used in History at A-Level where students were given nine different possible reasons as to why the Roundheads won the Civil War (control of London, better finances, etc.). Students then discuss each of these reasons in turn and decide which one is the main or most important one (top point of the diamond), then find two other similarly high-ranking ones all the way through the diamond, ending with the least important. You often find students are quickly able to identify or agree on the most or least important ideas but it is the ranking of the middle ones that often produces the most fruitful discussions.

It is interactive because if you place the ideas on cards students can move them around and they discuss and hopefully deepen their knowledge. Making the cards may seem like a wasted effort but believe me it is worth it. Students are much more willing to be flexible and change their ideas in discussions with others if they are able to reposition the cards, whereas if they are required to write down their opinions they are less likely to complete the task with the consideration required. Students very often make up their mind too quickly and refuse to change it once they have committed pen to paper.

Make this task more challenging by omitting one or more of the ideas or reasons on the diamond and asking students to come up with one themselves. Also once the students (in groups of no more than three – this means everybody has a real chance to contribute) have thrashed out their reasons and agreed on a ranking, it is interesting to put them with another group of three and ask them to reorganise their diamonds by asking both groups to come up with a single diamond or to explore their different ideas.

Diamond ranking can be used particularly well in English lessons, for example, by giving students a number of characters and asking who is most crucial to the play, most to blame for the tragic ending, most deserving of the audience's sympathy? Or with a number of quotations and asking students to select which of them they would find of most use for answering a particular question.

Thinking point

What about your subject? Could diamond ranking be a jewel in your teaching crown? How might you use it and would it be a suitable activity?

2. Go for five!

Ask pairs of students to come up with five ideas or examples connected with a particular topic. This quick and focused activity really gets the brain going and if you ask them to use sticky notes then you can quickly collect in a few of them and see what they've done. This sort of immediate recall is a good way of getting students going and makes them sit up and take notice right at the start of the lesson. Hopefully they are at their most alert and receptive – or if they aren't, after this activity they soon will be.

3. **Photographs, graphs, pictures or puzzles**

Show students an arresting picture, photograph or graph that is connected to the topic. Ask them to discuss what they are being shown; try to make the discussion stimulating and challenging by really making them think. Perhaps show them a picture they can only partially see or ask them to devise five further questions that they would like to ask about the resource. Make sure you give students enough information to complete the task but be careful about giving away too much information in your explanation. This is a common trait in a teacher who wants to 'tell all' instead of engaging their students in an interactive fashion and really making them think.

4. **Prediction**

A good way to kick things off at the start of the lesson is to get students to speculate about what might happen next. This is an important point. For example, perhaps show a video clip, picture or a short section of text that relates to the area you are studying. Think very carefully about what it is you are trying to teach the students and select an activity that leads on directly from this. As a prompt ask the students to use their knowledge about the topic to speculate about what might happen next and to give their reasons for this.

5. **Ask a big question**

An engaging way to get the students thinking is to pose a statement and ask them to discuss it, for example: 'It is always wrong to kill' or 'London was the most important reason why the Roundheads won the Civil War' or 'Tennessee Williams expects us to side with Stella in the play not Blanche'. These can provoke really fruitful discussions, especially if you ask students to pin them down with reasons. It can also be a good idea to ask them what they already know about this topic.

6. **Cloze procedure**

Display or hand out a piece of sustained written text that has some of the key words removed. Try to pick key pieces of vocabulary that the students have come across in a previous lesson as this is a good way to test their recall.

The challenge for students is to decide which word should fit into the space. This task can be differentiated by providing a list of words for the students to choose from. It is clearly more challenging if the word list option is not given. Key vocabulary used in diagrams and maps can also be revised in this way. In some subjects such as RE, English and History, cloze procedure can be a strategy used to help students become more discriminating or adventurous with their choice of vocabulary. For example, ask students to select a word that best supports the next point in their argument or creates the best atmosphere in a piece of descriptive writing. In these cases there are no right or wrong answers, but students can be challenged to give thoughtful, reasoned decisions behind their word choices. This can also stimulate an interesting classroom discussion to decide the relative merits of each word.

Plan ahead

When you develop any excellent resources, think about getting them laminated and keeping them carefully with your other lesson ideas. Remember, not every lesson starter depends upon thirty sets of coloured cards. You certainly haven't got the time to make these regularly and your department probably won't have the money for endless laminating. It is worth making some really good resources for key topics and be prepared to lend these to other members of the department. They will be grateful for the loan and you are bound to find some useful resources flocking your way in return. Don't think that you have to be original and generate every last resource yourself. Training courses run by your local authority or commercial companies such as Osiris Educational (www.osiriseducational.co.uk) and Lighthouse (www.lighthouse.tv) always have a wealth of ready-to-use teaching materials provided on their courses.

Remember to network and trade your best ideas with other staff teaching the same subject. Check out websites – such as the Times Educational Supplement (www.tes.co.uk) and follow the link to resources – which have free resources and investigate your subject area's teaching association. Importantly, remember that a dynamic interactive start to the lesson doesn't necessarily depend on lots of bespoke resources. A key question or a photocopy of a student's work can be just as engaging and intriguing as endless coloured cards which are time consuming to produce. The effectiveness of the starter depends on how you phrase your instructions and how you link the activity to the learning in the lesson. So, go on, make an effort to really think about the way you start your lessons next week. You may be surprised at the effect it has.

Reflection moment

What range of activities do I use to start my lessons off in a lively and interactive way? Why not have a go at the Teaching Strategies questionnaire (p. 90). This is designed to make you think about the different teaching strategies there are. However we know that we all have favourites, but we should increase the range we employ. Use the questionnaire to gauge your current range – perhaps compare your answers with everyone else in your department. Just think, if you each pooled one idea you would end up with a much larger selection. Consider which of these you use and which you don't currently employ but might prove to be an engaging and appropriate learning technique for your students.

What three dynamic activities do I use to kick off my lessons?

1.

2.

3.

Next week make a special effort with the start of your lessons. Try three different ways of kicking off your lessons and review how they go. Perhaps make some different resources or consider not taking the register right at the start of the session. What three new techniques will I try out?

1

2.

3.

How did it go?

Review the three new starters. Did getting the lesson off to a flying start make for any benefit during the rest of the period? How did students respond? Perhaps if you are feeling brave get somebody in to watch you and ask them to focus on the beginning of the lesson. They will be able to scan and see much more of what is happening, which can be very reassuring. Active starters are often noisy as students are doing things and learning. It can be tempting to shush them too much or worry about this – another pair of eyes can tell you whether this is lively on-task talk or otherwise!

Share and steal

Make sure if you have invested time or effort to create new resources, or if you have thought of some new teaching techniques, that you share these with others. Then you can ask them for some return favours for your next lesson starters which will help you build a larger repertoire of interesting and dynamic ideas.

Chapter 6

Asking the Right Questions

> If a student gives a response you hadn't considered before, don't shut them up – explore it! Never be embarrassed if you don't know something in front of a class. Look it up or work it out together – it shows them that you don't have to be infallible either.
>
> Ian Kirby, acting head of department and teacher, Roade School and Sports College

This chapter explores the important skill of effective questioning within the classroom. Sounds simple enough doesn't it? You'd think so, but questioning skills are one of the most important but underappreciated skills in the teacher's toolkit. Learning how to ask questions well can help students' learning, inform you of their progress and create a real dynamic in your lesson.

Interested in learning more? Consider how you ask questions and what happens when you do so. Does a forest of hands shoot up? Is everybody expected to contribute or do you get the same students eager to answer each time? If the answer is the latter, have you thought about different ways of involving more class members and getting a better quality of response?

One of the ways to do this is giving students longer to answer a question. Did you know the average teacher asks a question and then expects a response in less than a second? Imagine yourself as a student for a minute, no half a second, in fact. Would you actually bother to respond to the question, or might you perhaps let someone else do the work, one of the keen 5 per cent who actually manage to get their hand up that quickly? How involved would you really be if this is the case?

Asking better questions

Consider asking a slightly more challenging question and expect students to discuss it in pairs before asking for contributions. Asking students in pairs to think of five reasons why Macbeth is a villain is more challenging and demands their involvement much more than merely asking for a series of individual contributions asking for a single reason. Inviting students to think of five reasons (and then rank order them) leads to them extending their thinking and considering more carefully the question set.

It also makes the point that you expect *all* students to become involved in the lesson. There is no room for the slouch or idler when a teacher says, 'In a minute I'm going to select one of the pairs to report back on their reasons'. By allowing students to verbally rehearse their ideas with a partner usually results in a much better quality of response. Chatting over things even in five minutes with a partner can give students important thinking time and it allows them to discount the silly first response that often comes to mind. How often have you asked students for a response and before you actually finished ('Who can give me . . .?') several hands have shot up? I always used to complete the question by saying 'a million pounds' but the point is that many younger students are so keen to participate that they may not be thinking about the answer much at all – it is actually just a race to be the person who gets their hand up first. You can also have the other scenario where there is such a lack of volunteers that when a student does give a hasty and incorrect response it can be hard to put them right. This doesn't help anybody.

Think about how you use and manage incorrect responses and unexpected answers. It is important *if* there is a correct answer that any misconceptions in the students' understanding are corrected, otherwise confusion ensues and misunderstandings become accepted as fact.

I observed a Year 7 lesson while seated on the back row with some likely lads. During the lesson (on poetry) a typical question and answer session followed the reading of the poem. The teacher asked the class which poetic technique the poet had used in a particular line. As quick as a flash a hand went up in the front row and a boy answered 'metaphor'. The teacher shook her head – this was clearly the wrong answer. The boy next to him immediately put his hand up and said hopefully 'simile?'. The teacher agreed and the lesson moved on. I spoke to the boys next to me to see if they knew why the answer was simile and why metaphor was incorrect. The boy on my left said to me, 'Ah Ben (the simile boy) always knows the answer' – as if that explained everything. My friend on the other side of me looked more knowingly and whispered a helpful tip: 'With *English* teachers if it isn't a *simile* it's a *metaphor* and if it's not a *metaphor* it is a *simile*!' as if that explained everything. It was abundantly clear that the two boys – although making up their own rules – had no real idea of the difference.

I waited for the teacher to clarify or push Ben into explaining *why* it was a simile and not a metaphor – but the lesson moved on regardless. I didn't manage to get to the front of the classroom to see if Ben really knew why it was a simile or if he'd simply adopted the other boys' rule of thumb

– just give the teacher the opposite word. In this teacher's lesson it was a failsafe strategy. Although a questioning session had gone on, it appeared to have served very little effective purpose. Although we are always keen to move on with our lesson, we neglect the follow up or 'Does anyone else agree with this and can they tell me why?' question at our peril.

Correcting misunderstandings and handling the wrong answer

There are of course moments when we must correct misunderstandings and we must do so with sensitivity and regard for the individual concerned. Answering questions and putting your hand up in a lesson is a risk for a pupil. An amazing teacher should strive to encourage all students to answer, participate and take risks when answering questions. We need to make any amendments or corrections with tact, clarity and courtesy. *We* set the tone in our classroom and if we are to get the best out of our students there must be a supportive climate that provides the confidence for individuals in the class to answer and comment and contribute on each others' responses.

Recently I observed a lesson in which the teacher said (allowing very little thinking time): 'Nick, you're intelligent. What is the answer to x?' (Hoping I imagine for a showcase 'perfect' answer to her question.) Nick responded with an answer that was correct, but divergent and totally unexpected. The teacher immediately said in an angry tone: 'No. That's wrong! That wasn't a very clever answer. Concentrate better young man!' Later in the lesson I asked Nick why he had given the answer he did – to which he gave a very thoughtful and developed response. Had the teacher thought to ask a follow-up question she would have seen it was a particularly intelligent response – much more so in fact than the answer she was looking for.

An amazing teacher can't be expected to predict all the possible range of answers that students might give – however an amazing teacher is open minded and is sometimes known to stop mid-flow to respond to an answer, 'Oh I hadn't thought of that!' or 'I'm not sure – can you tell me a little more about that?' or occasionally, 'Well done – you are the first person I've taught who has ever said that'. Try this, when you genuinely mean it, and see the student's confidence grow – just look at the body language! An amazing teacher also welcomes the occasional intelligent interruption during the lesson. A comment I've *never* heard from an amazing teacher – but I have from the less confident teacher – is: '*I* ask the questions, not you!' or even worse, 'I'm the one with the degree'. An amazing teacher doesn't always know all of the answers – but they can find out (and there's no shame in admitting this to the students). They know that if students are sufficiently involved to want to ask a question, then they are showing their participation, engagement and interest in the lesson. What could be better than that?

Strategies for better student involvement

Think about how you want students to respond. Traditionally students put their hands up, but this isn't always the best way. Try a 'no hands up' policy whereby you expect all students to participate and the students know that you can ask any one of them at any time. Students are likely to be more alert and pay more attention if they know they can be called on to respond at any time by the teacher. You can also make sure that everyone participates by choosing individuals to respond. You can still differentiate by choosing who to answer each specific question.

Have you tried using mini-whiteboards? These are great for questions at the end of a lesson. Consider getting students to write their answers on these so that when you are checking factual recall, the whole class can show you their responses at once. You need to be quite stern in setting out the rules, for example, 'After a count of five you must all hold up your whiteboards'. If you have a learning support assistant in the lesson consider enlisting their help so they can monitor the students' responses to see who has answered the questions correctly and which concepts are causing difficulty for the whole class, groups or individuals. You can reinforce these aspects more successfully after whole class feedback.

Think about the types of questions you are posing. Consider asking a colleague to focus on your use of questions when they observe you teaching a lesson. Are most of your questions short, closed, factual questions such as 'What is the symbol for lead?', 'What is the word to describe the person who tells a story?' or 'How many wives did Henry VIII have?' If so, think about giving your students the opportunity to think more deeply about the subject by asking more open-ended questions.

Finally, watch out for playing the dangerous game of asking questions which only invite students to guess what is in the individual teacher's mind. For example, I have seen lessons where there need not be a specific answer, but the teacher phrases the question in such a way that the whole class is left rubbing their heads trying to think of the particular word the teacher has in mind. For example, 'What word could we use to describe George? It starts with an S?' (Really, this happens all too often, and even after having taught *Of Mice and Men* six times I was still scratching my head. What word was she possibly thinking of?) Several good suggestions by students were ignored, 'No it begins with S'. How much better it would have been to have asked pairs to think of five adjectives to describe George and then select four pairs to feedback their best one. And as for the word beginning with S, I can't for the life of me remember it anyway.

If you want to improve your use of questions consider the top tips below.

Thinking point

Have you tried:

- Planning out your questions before the lesson? Try jotting them down on a sticky note.
- Asking a range of questions – closed and open?
- Getting students to rehearse ideas in pairs?
- Asking students to 'think of five'?
- Putting the big question on the board?
- Ensuring everyone participates? Watch out for only asking specific individuals/sexes.
- Asking students if they can add to or extend their own or others' answers?
- Exploring misconceptions rather than glossing over them: 'But if *x* was true, what would happen . . .'?
- Giving students answers in the form of key words and asking them to devise the questions that go with them? It's a good plenary. If students can devise the

right question you can be sure they've understood the concept.

- Asking students to come up with their own questions for a topic? Perhaps start a question board where students can record these and you can draw on them in a plenary.

- Asking to watch a colleague's lesson and focus on their use of questioning? Look to see how many students are involved. What techniques do they use? How do they deal with misconceptions?

Next lesson I will try:

1.

2.

3.

When my lessons are being observed I will ask the observer to particulary focus on x connected with my questions.

Chapter 7

Amazing Group Work: Making it Happen

I always think about what it would be like to be in my own lesson. The key question I ask myself is: would I enjoy this lesson? I also like to keep it in mind that students have four or five other lessons per day; my aim is to make the lesson with me their best lesson of the day.

John Harris, head of English, Danetre School, Daventry

An amazing teacher knows that organising effective group work is a key teaching strategy and a test of effective classroom management. Managing group work is a tricky skill but one that is really worth mastering. When teachers trill out 'Get into groups', this can be the signal for some really high-quality interactions with a lot of meaningful work and high-focused activity – or an excuse for students to mess about, leaving the teacher frustrated and with the onset of a vicious headache.

Watch any skilled teacher manage group work effectively and it can appear to happen 'just by magic'. Students obediently and quietly move into groups, cooperatively start on the task and work in a focused and hardworking way all lesson. And yes, in the really successful group work lesson there's even time for the students to help you pack away, move furniture back and replace equipment. There's nothing like being caught all hot and flustered, dragging tables back into their places while clutching armfuls of glue sticks and coloured card, just as boisterous Year 11 barge into the classroom ready for the next lesson. Moreover in some group work lessons there's even the chance to get the students to review learning by means of an effective plenary. Allowing each group to feedback on their main findings is often an appropriate and satisfying end to the lesson.

So if all of the above is possible, then why is it that some group work lessons turn into a group 'chat' where the word 'work' seems distinctively lacking from the operations? There are seven golden rules for successful group work. Take the opportunity to watch some of your colleagues who have mastered it and look out for the strategies they use to make things move smoothly in their lessons and ensure that it is the students who are really working.

1. **Get the ground rules right**

   Group work is great because it puts the impetus on the students to do the work rather than relying on didactic teaching from the front. But in order for it to work you need to have effective classroom management. After all if the class won't be quiet when you are managing whole class feedback, then setting them off in groups is only going to be a recipe for disaster. You need to instil in the class some rules about their behaviour. Yes, they may be working in groups which will necessitate more discussion than usual but this does not mean shouting and excessive noise is allowed. There is a difference between the lively hum of activity and a full scale free-for-all! So keep a handle on the volume control and ensure you 'pull the class back' if they are getting too noisy. Also keep scanning the room for any off-task behaviour and if you spot any deal with the individual or stop the class for a moment.

2. Great expectations

Make sure you are clear about your expectations. Some students will happily wander about from group to group or use a more relaxed environment to start texting, chatting about last night's TV or doing a bit of revision for the French test next lesson: this is not on. Avoid problems by making it very clear what is expected and get any equipment sorted out at the start of the lesson (or make one sensible person per table responsible for collecting what the table needs at the start of the lesson *and* putting it back at the end). Make it very clear initially what your rules are and keep monitoring them as the lesson develops. It is a mistake to think that you can sit back and relax when group work is going on. You need to scan the room very regularly to check that everyone is on task and that the lesson is moving forward in a purposeful way.

3. Control by non-verbal communication

Drama teachers often use very effective non-verbal communication for catching students' attention when they want to bring them back or issue instructions when students are engaged in a task. Explain to students that instead of bellowing at them you will raise your arm when you want silence and when they see this they should stop talking and do likewise. This can silence a room in seconds – without the need for a raised voice. Teachers with effective classroom management and presence can also exaggerate pushing down a volume control to indicate they need the sound quietening down. These may sound unlikely – and they do need mastering – but try it and persist: it works!

4. **Effective lesson planning**

If you think, 'Oh they can do group work today' and see it as a way of avoiding proper planning then the lesson will descend into chaos. You will need to plan much more rigorously for group work; if students are going to work more independently and cooperatively then it must be very clear what they are doing, the resources should be excellent and you ought to give some thought to the layout of the classroom.

It is much better if the room is already set up for group work before the students arrive, either by doing it yourself or by getting your tutor group or previous class to arrange the desks. That way your class will be able to focus on listening to your instructions rather than fighting about moving desks and chairs.

Be careful to chunk your lesson. Ensure that students (initially anyway) aren't working in groups without a change of task for longer than twenty minutes. Make it clear what the outcome of the lesson is – maybe the discussion will be used to write a debate for a speaking and listening assessment, as a role play in front of the class or as a springboard for making a page of revision notes. It should have a clear purpose and this needs to be signalled to the class before they start.

5. **Delegate different responsibilities**

Think about what you are getting them to do. Are all ten groups going to investigate Rome? Is this a good idea? What about dividing up the task or getting different groups to investigate different aspects of the topic? If I know that my group is the only one investigating Iceland / making a presentation on Juliet / studying van Gogh's *Sunflowers* paintings and we have to feedback to the rest of the class, then it is more likely that I will work harder rather than if the whole class is set an identical topic. Ensure that you build in time at the end, even if you haven't planned to do a full feedback – at least make sure you have time to summarise the work done. Signal where you will be starting from next time – oh yes, and put the tables back.

6. Clear instructions

Give clear instructions and repeat them if necessary. Write them on the board to reinforce them and so that students can easily reference them. Ensure that students know exactly what they have to do. If there are eight stages, for example, consider only explaining the ones they will be doing today. Check that students are nodding. Ask a couple to clarify what they are doing and tell the rest of the class. If there is uncertainty explain again and in a different way. Make sure they know why they are doing something and for how long. Don't say, 'Off you go . . . you have the whole lesson.' Say, 'You have twenty minutes to get the first task done and then I will be stopping you.' (If they are working really hard you can review this, but you are telling them you expect them to work!) If you think at any time students aren't clear, then stop them, clarify and continue. Give clear instructions. Repeat them if necessary!

7. Group size and group make-up

If the group is any larger than five then some students will go off task. Yep, it is a certainty. Unless you are a group work pro then keep it small. Four is ideal – you need to make sure that everybody pulls their weight and feels a responsibility for the outcome. If there are too many students in a group then some shirkers won't bother and they will either not learn anything and/or be disruptive. A teacher I observed had a group work disaster and when asked about her group sizes she still insisted that 'eleven wasn't unmanageable!' It is. If you have larger groups then you will need to give roles within them. Put some thought into deciding on the groups before the lesson – if you let students always work with friends then some groups might not be effective. Moreover students need to learn to work well with other people. *You* decide on the groupings. This is also an effective way to differentiate: even within a top group there will be levels and degrees of ability. Giving students of a similar standard the chance to work together is a really good idea and you can subtly decide on the most appropriate topic or give them slightly more challenging questions.

Thinking point

Managing effective group work takes skill and experience. It needs practice. Pick a class that you work well with and try it. Remember you can build up to it. You could plan for fifteen minutes of group work at the end of a lesson (that way if all goes awry, it's not long to the bell) or start with fifteen minutes of group work to generate ideas for essays. Build up to a whole lesson and experiment with what works well with your class. Choose your time carefully: Friday afternoon with bottom set Year 9 after PE might be just asking for trouble, or if properly structured might really engage them. Experiment, but remember the rules: clear expectations, precise outcomes and do remember to leave time to tidy the furniture at the end of the lesson.

Reflection moment

- Have all classes taken part in group work recently? What have been the successes and are there any issues?
- How do you ensure that all students are involved in the group work you undertake?
- What strategies do you have for making the format and groupings different and avoiding the possibility for things to become mundane?
- What new ideas or strategies are you intending to trial out? It is always a good idea to try out some new ideas from other classes or have a look at the group work strategies below.

What is working well?

1.

2.

3.

What I plan to improve or try out in the next two weeks:

1.

2.

3.

Different group work strategies

An amazing teacher is always looking to add to their repertoire, finding and trying out new teaching techniques.

Below are some commonly used group work strategies that can be well matched to suit a range of different learning outcomes. When choosing a new technique remember it can be very useful to watch a colleague use it first; this enables you to talk over any potential issues.

Think about the class you are working with – different techniques need different levels of cooperation and autonomy by the students. Establishing new patterns of behaviour takes time. Make sure your instructions are clear and you are very precise about what you are going to be doing: write down instructions to help you and them. There are sometimes teething problems when starting a new type of group work – bear with it. If students need to become more independent there may well be resistance and you may need to spend time explaining and setting out ground rules on the first occasion. This is an investment and it is well worth persevering.

Below are various ideas that have worked for me. This is not an exhaustive list – you will find that teachers in your school have other worthwhile ideas to share. Remember, think carefully about what you want students to learn first, then think about which of the following types of group work are likely to best support this and suit the needs of your class.

Pyramiding

Students first of all work as individuals or in pairs on a particular question or part of an investigation. They are then asked to join with another pair or a third member of the group is added. Next they are asked to refine their response in the light of the new input or to progress with the next stage of the investigation. The addition of new group members and additional tasks or areas for students to think about keeps them focused, allows for active involvement and encourages participation by the entire group.

Role plays

Students are asked to respond 'in role' as particular characters or people in a given situation. You need to allow them sufficient time to prepare for this. It is also a good idea to model this behaviour first of all, by acting 'in role' to show them how it is done. It is essential to set out clear guidance and to point out clearly when the class is 'in role'.

Speed dating

(You will need to change the title if you are working with younger students or in a single-sex school.) Students are given a very limited and specific time (five minutes or less) to explain their idea or give their response to the person next to them, listen to their view and then move briskly on. The room is best set out with rows of students facing each other and a timekeeper (usually the teacher) is needed to keep things focused and to a tight pace. Clear instructions such as 'Row 1, move one seat to the right *now*' are needed to keep things moving and the students working under pressure. This technique is particularly useful for helping students revise topics or when you want them exposed to a large number of different responses.

Snowballing

Groups (usually about five students) work on a particular topic, area of responsibility or question. They are given a tight time limit and very clear instructions. Each student has a number. After a set time period students move groups, so that there is one student from each group in the new 'hub'. Then each student 'fills in' the other students in the group with the information they have gathered thereby ensuring that everybody is up-to-date with the new information and also that each student has taken responsibility and a role in doing this.

Messengers

Students are allocated to groups and each group works on a particular question or area. When the task is completed or after a particular time period, one person from each group is selected as a 'messenger' and they go to another group to share what they have done and to get a response from the new group. The messenger then returns to the original group to share the findings. This is a useful way of boosting students' independence and allowing them to develop the difficult skill of speaking to a group, taking a response from the group and then feeding this back. Some time should be allowed so that the group can respond to the messenger's feedback and add or alter their work accordingly.

Chapter 8

Plenary Perfect

> "The most satisfying part of a lesson? For the students, an opportunity to demonstrate knowledge and enthusiasm. For me, that adrenaline buzz moment, feeling like I have achieved my aims.
>
> Kate Lewis, Advanced Skills Teacher
> Arthur Mellows Village College"

Why is the skill of managing a perfect plenary a key part of the amazing teacher's toolkit? Firstly let us consider what makes a really good plenary and consider why we need them at all. The idea of a plenary is a way of seeing how much the students have learnt and a chance to pull all of the learning together as a summary. Imagine for a moment we didn't have a plenary – what might the structure of a lesson look like and why would the deficit matter? Well, hopefully we'd still have a focused and engaging start to the lesson – an amazing teacher knows they need to 'hook' students' attention right from the off. Somewhere in the lesson – not necessarily at the very start – the learning intentions or objectives would be explained so that students know where they are going and why their learning is important. Then we might have some brief teacher explanation (not overlong or students lose focus and switch off) to introduce the main ideas and to start students off on their learning. The main body of the lesson is usually broken into 'chunks' because it is often the case that setting students off on overlong tasks that give them too much unstructured time leads to a slowing down of the work rate and a lack of pace. At the end of the lesson we might set homework and send the students off to their next lesson – job done! Until the next class comes through the door . . .

It is probably at the end of the lesson where the need for a good plenary is most obvious. How can an amazing teacher judge the effectiveness of the students' learning if their progress is not reviewed at the end of the lesson? Reviewing how well all students have met their learning objectives – perhaps looking and sharing at some examples of their work – is one way of seeing if the lesson has been a success, or not. It also gives an opportunity to review all the learning: Has everybody grasped everything? Do some aspects need further consolidation at the start of the next lesson? Was it pitched at the right level or could the lesson have been made more challenging? It is clear that it is important to have a plenary – however it need not always be at the end of the session.

Why we need to review learning throughout the lesson

Think for a moment about some of the downsides of always having the plenary right at the end of the lesson. Aside from some of the practicalities, such as the fact that teachers often do not leave enough time to review learning properly, what happens if it transpires that the students really didn't understand a task and made little progress? Obviously this can be addressed in the next lesson, but amazing teachers know that building in mini-plenaries – midway through the lesson after a particular task – is one of the best ways of working out how students are progressing and whether the lesson is moving in the right direction. This can put a potentially unsuccessful lesson right back on track.

Managing an effective plenary takes planning and confidence. Teachers have a tendency to want to push on to the next task without allowing sufficient time to review progress. I have also observed many perfunctory plenaries at the end of a lesson where all that actually happens is the teacher reads off the lesson objective from the board – or even worse, just tells the students what they have been *doing* rather than *learning*. Sometimes they go even further and say, 'So you've met the all of the learning objectives' (smug look directed at the observer). I always have difficulty in these lessons in restraining myself from shouting out: 'Don't tell me what *you* think they have learnt. Let *them* tell you and prove to you what they actually have learnt!' Also it is incredibly boring for students to be told yet again by the teacher what they *should* have learnt – there are so many more interesting ways to do this! Remember, a good plenary should be as interactive and as engaging as the rest of the lesson, where all the students review what they have learnt and you as a teacher are aware of the next steps for learning. A good plenary doesn't just consolidate learning in that one lesson; it provides feedback for the teacher across a period of time and offers the chance to resolve any student misconceptions.

There are a wide number of strategies for conducting an effective plenary. Doubtless you will have your favourites (as long as reading the lesson objectives from the board isn't one of them). An amazing teacher knows however, the value of ringing the changes, keeping it fresh and using the strategy that best fits the learning you are trying to review.

Thinking point

- Do you review learning at the end of lesson?
- Think about the lessons you have taught recently. How do you know the learners made good progress?
- What different strategies do you use to make your plenaries more interesting and interactive?
- When you conduct a plenary are all students calm and in the right frame of mind? Do you give them enough time to actually *think* about what learning has happened in the lesson?

Try:

- Planning opportunities to involve and allow students to reflect on their learning midway through the lesson.
- Involving students in leading parts of the plenary. Try this with a class you are really confident with and that has some keen and well-motivated students. Arrange for them to conduct a quiz, lead a summary or set a challenge to assess how well the others have learnt.
- Having a look at the suggestions below for effective plenaries – be brave and try out at least three new strategies.

Strategies for effective plenaries

Below are some of my favourite strategies for managing a successful plenary. The list isn't exhaustive and you should also look out for tips from colleagues. It is often the case that teachers in particular subject areas have favourite approaches but it is worth sharing these with departments in other parts of the school for some new ideas.

- Ask students some questions on the topic and get them to use mini-whiteboards to hold up their answers. This is a simple and effective way to see how many have 'got it'. It also gives a better indication of whole class progress than just asking one or two students.

- Show some work with a deliberate error in it. Get the students to correct and improve it using what they have learnt.

- Do a quick quiz on key terms or vocabulary. Divide the class in half and use it as a light-hearted competition.

- Use the opportunity to share some good work you have found in the lesson. Make sure that all students can hear and see it. Ask the class to respond critically (but supportively) by picking out what works well and what could be improved. This avoids the 'mumble and then read out' plenary which can be both dull and a waste of time. Invest in a visualiser or scan students' work so it can be easily seen.

- Ask some probing questions which students must answer in pairs. Get them not only to recall information but to relate it to previous learning: 'In what ways is Athens similar and different to Rome?', 'Give me five similarities between Juliet and her mother?' Questions like these will encourage deeper thinking and allow bigger links to be made to the overall topic.

- Ask students to summarise what they have learnt in thirty words – handy if you've just spent an hour teaching them Act V of *Hamlet* or how the heart works. Share some of them with the class. What has been left out? Which is best? Why?

- Ask students to tell you three things they learnt today – and two things they want to know next.

- Ask students to write 'five things you need to know about . . .' as a way of summarising what they have learnt – so the five most important facts about aerobic fitness, the First World War, the storyline of *Of Mice and Men* and so on. You can then encourage them to debate which is the most important. This will lead to them reflecting in a critical way.

- Put some key words or facts from the lesson on the board such as dates, names, places, etc. Ask the students to make up the question that goes with it. So if you put: '1095' on the board the answer the students give might be: 'When was the First Crusade?' It is possible for there to be range of questions and it really makes students think.

- Get students to share their work with a partner and allow them to pick out two specific strengths and one clear target to work on.

- Ask students to come up with five tough questions and answers on the subject using their books. Then groups take turns quizzing each other. Can they answer each others' hard questions?

- Give students a very short task that will exemplify what they have learnt. So if they have been learning how to describe Monet's paintings show them a different painting and say they have got five minutes to explain the techniques used in three sentences.

- What if? Ask the students to consider 'what if' and explain their thoughts and reasons. So if they have been studying John Steinbeck's novel, 'What would be missing if Slim wasn't in the novel?' or 'What would have been the result if the Aztecs had had horses?

- Students learn things in different ways so give them opportunities to use diagrams, pictures, words or rhyme to make up a way of remembering something. Perhaps you have been studying the Elizabethan world and its hierarchy. Ask students to draw a simple diagram to reflect this. Encourage some to demonstrate on the board and it will allow them to explain their reasoning.

Thinking point

Remember, a plenary should give you the opportunity to see what the students have mastered and what still needs to be developed. Don't be afraid to ask them, 'What three things did you learn today?' but also what still needs to be reinforced. Make sure that you take note of the students' responses and ensure that you clarify and revisit any areas of learning they haven't yet secured.

What is working well?

1.

2.

3.

What I plan to improve or try out in the next two weeks:

1.

2.

3.

Chapter 9

Handy Hints for Homework

Can you remember completing homework when you were at school? What were your experiences like? It is probable that as a successful teacher you were probably relatively good at homework. No doubt you will have discovered that unfortunately not all of your charges share the same dedication in completing and handing it in. But this is not always the fault of the student – other factors often come into sway. Many teachers are poor at setting homework – how hard can it be, you think? Bad practice and general thoughtlessness in the setting of work can make the difference between homework being finished to a good standard or being attempted at all. Yes, as teachers we bear the main responsibility if students in our class fail to adopt good homework habits.

An amazing teacher sets homework in an effective and timely fashion. They know to avoid setting it so it is due in the next day – some students are involved in various activities or have commitments after school. We naturally feel that *our* subject is the most important – but students often complain, and with good reason, that many teachers frequently set similar deadlines resulting in an excessive workload. Obviously you need to follow your school's homework timetable for your subject, but being aware when other huge deadlines are looming is important especially as the pressure cranks up in the GCSE years.

Homework hell

Can you remember being given homework that infuriated or frustrated you as a student? Sometimes teachers are simply unaware of the repercussions of the work they have set. When I was 11, an English teacher set homework telling us to 'copy down your favourite poem' – the only poem I could find in my house was the immensely long 'The Walrus and the Carpenter' from Lewis Carroll's *Through the Looking-Glass*. It took me hours to painstakingly copy down all eighteen verses. Unfortunately I also had some confusion over the task and believed that we were also meant to memorise it – that was a stressful weekend I can tell you! Until this day – if you can get me drunk enough – I can recite a near perfect rendition of the first five verses (there was a limit to my memory skills at 11) but the actual purposeful learning behind it seems slim at best.

It appeared to be homework for homework's sake. It might have been better to have presented us with an anthology of poems to select from, thereby ensuring that we at least had a decent choice and were reading new material. Simply copying out your favourite poem brings no new learning, aside from a ruddy great blister on the index finger! Less tedious work, but better thought and learning would have been involved if we had been asked to copy out our favourite two lines from a poem and then actually *explain* what we liked about them. There would have been less physical effort (mindless copying out). However there would have been certainly much more thought involved and the task would have helped to sharpen our poetry reading skills, which was presumably the point of the task.

There are of course other factors that come into play when setting homework. We need to be very aware of the chaotic and difficult home lives of some of the students we teach. When I started teaching – in an average comprehensive in a relatively affluent area near Reading – I was surprised by the complex lives of some students. One lovely student had to live half the week with her mother and then move house (sometimes on different days) to a completely different area to live with her father. There was no hope of her simply popping back if she had forgotten a book. Her organisational skills at 13 were impressive, but in the days before portable technology some degree of sympathy was needed when she occasionally slipped up and genuinely forgot a piece of work. Eventually, allowing her a shelf in one of my cupboards to store things helped a little.

Many students live in overcrowded accommodation and simply lack privacy or a quiet space to complete homework; others have parents or carers who have no interest in them and their studies. Some students' lack of access to the internet, books, television, newspapers or other basic resources can make some simple sounding 'research' homework very difficult for them. However, I am not saying that we should not set such homework; we just need to be very mindful of the resources and support some students do not have. The work we set needs to be fair to all and unnecessary barriers to completing it should be avoided.

Some schools offer 'homework clubs', which is not quite the oxymoron you might think. These offer the opportunity for helpful teacher support – and even just the haven of some peace and quiet and a flat surface on which to work can make a real difference. Some refreshments, the availability of ICT and access to a supportive adult can be invaluable in helping students (you would be surprised how often homework is not completed not because students misunderstand what they need to do but because they lack ICT equipment and basic resources such as paper or coloured pens).

They can also be crucial in helping students who lack organisational skills to establish good study habits. Even if your school does not offer such a timetabled provision it can be a good idea to dedicate part of a lunchtime or a couple of hours after school once a week when students know that you will be on hand in your classroom to offer help and advice. By making it clear that you are available for support you are also tightening the net around those students who will simply turn up without their homework claiming they 'didn't know what to do'.

Why students don't complete homework

One of the reasons that students don't complete homework at all or fail to complete it to a good standard is because of how it is set and what is done with it afterwards. On many occasions homework is set in the last frantic minutes of a busy lesson when students have mentally already left the room and the teacher is trying to cram in too many instructions into too short a space of time. Students often don't get time to copy down the details of the work properly and inevitably the deadline is missed off either the instructions or the note making.

If we want to make sure that students complete homework with due care and attention then we need to set it more efficiently. Time should be taken so that students are absolutely clear what they are being asked to do, the deadline and what a teacher is expecting from a good piece of work. Sufficient time should be allowed for questions and for recording it into homework planners. Help or guidance should be given to students with special needs to ensure that it has been recorded properly. (This might include having it recorded for them or pre-printed on a slip of paper that is stuck in their planner.) There is no rule that states homework should be given in the mad rush at the end of the lesson – wouldn't it be far better to set it in the middle of the lesson or even at the start? If you have further lessons before the deadline then timely verbal reminders will help students to keep the fact that they need to complete homework for you in the forefront of their minds.

Thinking point

- Do you leave sufficient time to set homework in your lessons?
- Does the homework you give consolidate or further the learning of your students?
- Do you have effective methods for praising good homework and following up late homework?
- Do you make use of the homework that you have set in lessons so that students feel it is worth completing?
- Do you set homework according to the school policy and timetable?
- Do you have a wide variety of homework tasks rather than just 'finishing off' classwork?

Harnessing motivation

If you have ever been asked to do something for a particular date and have worked hard to meet the deadline, you will know how galling it is when the person who has set the work fails to ask for it – or grants liberal extension to those who haven't even bothered to complete it on time. If you do this when you set homework it undermines your professionalism and the value you place on the work. *If* homework is to be seen as a priority by your students then *you* have to value it and treat it in such a way that it has importance and adds to the relevance and learning of your lessons.

An amazing teacher knows what homework they have set for each class – and knows also when they have asked for it in, remembers to collect it and deals relentlessly with any slackers. You have to be organised – if you can't remember precisely what you have set, students will run rings around you. Use whatever strategies work for you, such as highlighting deadlines in your planner and having an orderly way of collecting in work, such as when students leave the room or as you take the register by asking students to bring their books up to the front desk and open them on the page that shows their work. Both of these will highlight those students who have completed it.

Excuses and issues with students need to be rigorously followed up on, but they should be not allowed to deflect or detract from the opening of your lesson. Avoid at all costs getting into a protracted discussion with such miscreants – instead do something that reminds you that you need to deal with them, such as collecting in their homework diaries or making a note of their names. Then deal with them in the last few minutes of the lesson, at breaktime or lunchtime – the inconvenience should be theirs. You will need to discover if there are genuine grounds why the work has not been done, such as illness or other issues; in these cases your students should have been instructed to bring a note from home or their tutor. Students will only adopt good attitudes towards homework if you make it matter to them – and if they know you will hunt them down in a relentless fashion if they fail to do it.

Why set homework at all?

We also need to think about the purpose of the homework – before we set it. It should benefit the students. There is no reason why it needs to involve masses of writing – so use your imagination. Sometimes asking students to think of questions they would like answered or to discuss a topic and find out others views can yield useful information.

However, be careful how you set things up, as asking students to research a wide topic often results in them downloading lots of material from the internet and not even reading it or discriminating between the information. If you set research homework perhaps set a series of questions students should investigate or ask them to summarise what they have found in twenty words. The advantage is that not only will you have much less to mark but the actual learning will be a deeper and richer experience for the students. Make sure the work you set is appropriate for the ability levels of *all* of the students you teach. It might be necessary to set different homework for different groups or to ensure that the scope of the work sufficiently caters for various abilities. Make sure you don't just automatically heap extra work onto the very able students – making them work through low-level work first will only be demotivating and a waste of time.

Homework can be enjoyable – but think about a range of appropriate tasks. Be aware that although sometimes 'finishing off' tasks can be appropriate they sometimes can be vague and too dependent upon the individual student's level of effort. Be clear about what the success criteria is for the homework and make this obvious to the students.

In some very marking-heavy subjects less is sometimes more. I have seen a really good newly qualified teacher nearly in tears because she could not cope with the thirty top set students' very long (fourteen or so pages) 'short' stories. Not only were they long but they also weren't very good: lots of dialogue and thin description. In this case she should have taught a lesson in which she focused on teaching interesting writing skills, then set a homework that consolidated this skill; for example, asking them to write using a very limited number of words (fifty words maximum) where they improved and reworked an opening to a story by using detailed description and effective vocabulary. Some students will want to write much more and may even protest that they can't – but by making them focus in this way you will be ensuring a *quality* of response rather than a quantity. This strategy worked and meant that the teacher's marking load was more manageable and more importantly the homework did what it should: it improved the students' learning. This example shows that one of the most important criteria when setting homework is to identify exactly what you are trying to achieve and to ensure the homework does just this.

Reflection moment

Consider the homework you are setting.

- Does it refine and develop the students' skills? Tasks might involve improving or reworking a draft or taking into account the teacher's corrections to produce a better piece of work.

- Does it consolidate their knowledge (e.g. revising vocabulary for a test)? Bear in mind that students may not know the best way to learn facts and figures. Don't forget to give them tips and demonstrate how to do this. If you promise them a test make sure you deliver. Think about being creative too – perhaps asking students to design a test for each other. This is a really good way of checking their understanding; just make sure they provide the answers.

- Does it ask them to research or learn to use a resource (e.g. reference materials or the internet)? Asking students to conduct surveys and find out links between what they are learning and how it relates to the real world is also beneficial.

- Does it develop wider knowledge? Tasks that get students to explore the topic in ways that build on the lesson are useful. Homework opportunities can give students more time to immerse themselves in the task.

Remember, students will be more motivated by homework if it is seen to have a clear purpose. Make sure you give plenty of verbal praise and use the school reward system to bolster students' motivation and effective work. It is also crucial to be persistent in tracking down and ensuring that *all* students complete the homework you have set, whether in their own time or in detention. Amazing teachers are like Canadian Mounties – known for always 'getting their man'. Once students know that you will make it your mission to get their homework, and that it will be more effort to evade completing homework rather than just doing it, you will find that they will make the completion of *your* homework their first priority.

Section II

Assessment for Learning and the Amazing Teacher

Chapter 10

Assessment for Learning

How to Make it Happen in Your Lessons

Harnessing effective Assessment for Learning strategies is essential in developing the skills of an amazing teacher. Firstly we must consider the essence of effective Assessment for Learning and then think about how we manage these in the everyday classroom.

Assessment for Learning is the buzz term used in schools at the moment, but what exactly does it mean and why is it so important? It is certainly more than the latest educational gimmick. Assessment for Learning is defined as: 'the process of seeking and interpreting evidence for use by learners and their teachers to decide where the learners are in their learning, where they need to go and how best to get there' (Assessment Reform Group, 2002). In essence Assessment for Learning puts the learner – the student – at the heart of the learning process; it is about empowering individuals through good teaching so that students know their next learning steps and are able to progress effectively.

Marking and motivation

Thinking point

What do you think is the most useful in helping students to make effective progress:

1. Getting a numerical mark or grade on a piece of work?

2. Getting a written comment?

3. Getting a numerical/written grade and written comment?

Evidence from Paul Black and Dylan Wiliam (2004) shows that although students like to receive a numerical mark – particularly because it shows them where they are in the scheme of things – what helps them to really make progress is the written comment. This might be a surprise to some – surely a combination of written comment and grade is the ideal? Apparently not if you actually want the student to read your comments and take them in. I am sure we have all had the experience of getting feedback on something, perhaps a lesson observation or other piece of work, and once you have heard the judgement on whether your lesson is deemed good, outstanding or otherwise, there can be a tendency to switch off and not hear the finer details.

This is certainly the case with students. I know after teaching several classes of borderline students where motivation was an issue. If I returned an essay to them – even if I had written lots of positive and guiding comments – if it gained a grade D rather than a C it was dismissed and even on occasion screwed into a ball and thrown away as rubbish! As a prospective amazing teacher this really used to upset me. Hadn't I spent hours late at night lovingly writing helpful comments to move students on with their learning? It did not fare much better even if it gained the 'magic' grade C. Often these students (predominantly boys, I must say) would look at the grade, sigh with relief then turn around and chat to their neighbour. Despite the hours of marking, my helpful guidance would be neglected. Sometimes it seemed as if I might as well not have bothered; I wondered if there was a more effective way of getting students to act on and value my feedback.

Obviously we need to give students a very clear steer on where they are with their ability and attainment levels. It would be very unfair to give them lots of helpful advice on their work, which might make them think they were achieving at the highest levels, when in fact their achievements were rather more modest. But it is also true that once we write a numerical grade on work our students, like all of us, become blinkered. They see the grade and all it implies rather than the helpful comment

Getting students involved

It is good for students to understand the process of marking, especially using strategies such as peer- and self-assessment.

Neil Welsh, PE teacher, Prince William School, Oundle

What an amazing teacher needs to do when marking an important piece of work and providing a quality written response is to give students time to read, absorb and act on the information. They may also need to know what grade they received for a piece of work but there is nothing to

stop you holding back this information and giving it out in another lesson. If you can do this then there is much more chance that they will read carefully and take action on the information you have given. Students will certainly resist this at first and will doubtless clamour for 'my mark'; however, an amazing teacher knows that they sometimes need to remain resolute, even if it means resisting a whole class appeal and being seen as unpopular for a while. Stay strong on this point because you really are doing it for their own good.

How do we enable students to recognise where they are and what their next steps should be? Well the teacher certainly has a crucial role in the assessment progress. Often when we think about assessment, tests and exam results spring to mind – that is *summative assessment* which sums up and reflects what a learner has achieved in a final test or examination. Assessment for Learning focuses more on *formative assessment* – which is the range of feedback that a teacher gives to a student that helps them see the next steps in their learning. For example, a summative assessment might tell me that I have achieved 15 out of 20, or a grade E, while formative feedback would indicate what parts of the work has met the criteria, what I have done well and it would identify the next steps I need to take to improve my work.

Effective Assessment for Learning is about intervening *before* the students complete summative assessments (tests, exams, coursework, etc.) to help them discover what is working and what they need to do to make progress. It is about sharing information with students, empowering them and guiding them to the next step. It is only in this way that students can take responsibility for their own learning and ultimately improve.

Encouragingly, research by Dylan Wiliam and Paul Black in *Inside the Black Box* (2004) suggests that not only is formative assessment more effective than summative assessment, but it also encourages and motivates all students. The grade on our work is only a crude indication of whether we have passed or failed, whereas a meaningful comment that indicates our strengths and how we need to improve is more likely to encourage us. Formative assessment also implies that ability is not static and that whatever level you are at there is clear room for improvement.

Thinking point

- How often do you use summative or formative assessment in your lessons?
- When you use summative assessment, how do you make sure students know what they need to do to improve?
- What strategies do you have for managing the motivation of the low-achieving student or the student who seems to effortlessly gain full marks?
- How motivated are students by your marking? What do they like about it? What do they dislike about it? Have some conversations with your students and seek their views.
- To find out how successful assessment is in your lessons, ask students what they need to do to improve their work. The more exact and precise they are in their comments the more successful and useful your marking is.
- Take a look at some of the marking. Be honest. How far do the comments help students move on in their

learning and make better progress? How many of the comments relate specifically to the qualities of the work and what needs to be done to improve it?

What practical steps can you make to encourage Assessment for Learning strategies in your classroom? Ones that have worked well for me and that I see in successful lessons include:

- **Share the assessment criteria**

  Students often complete work without it being made explicit what the teacher is looking for. What skills are going to be rewarded? What level of detail is required? What needs to be included if I am aiming for a grade C, B or A? Make sure that you make these criteria clear to students and phrase them in easy-to-understand language. It is usually effective to write these in the form of bullet points on the board and to refer to them when you start the work. Ask students to check their own work and their partner's work against these criteria and refer to them again at the end of the lesson.

  Back in 2004, an Ofsted report commented that: 'Not enough students know what they need to do to improve their work.' Although we might hope things have changed since then, sadly in some classrooms this is still the case. Not so for the amazing teacher, I hear you cry, but we do need to be absolutely crystal clear not just what task we are setting students but what skill we are hoping they will master and how it will be evident if they are successful in achieving this. We also need to think of helpful strategies and check with students that they are as clear on the success criteria as we think they are.

Assessment for Learning has been an important strategy in raising achievement for a number of years now but sometimes this familiarity can cause problems in its effectiveness. We all feel well acquainted with the jargon of Assessment for Learning: we know we should be using 'objectives' rather than 'tasks' and talking about 'success criteria'. However, we need to make sure that by using the 'correct' terminology we don't fool ourselves into thinking that we are managing Assessment for Learning effectively when this is not actually the case.

As a Local Authority adviser I visited a school which assured me they were fully up to date with Assessment for Learning. It was embedded they said; they were exceptional. However the data and examination results seemed to indicate the opposite, but it was a chance observation that really highlighted the problem. Discussing data with a head of department in a classroom the following instructions on the whiteboard caught my eye. They read:

Objective: To complete pp. 34–36 Hodder

Target: To work in silence

Homework: Copy up last lesson's work

You can imagine what I thought of this! Aside from the fact that the objective was a task, rather than focusing on a skill the student should have been learning, it bothered me that an absent or sleeping student would be more likely to meet their target (being silent!) than a student who was engaged in a focused discussion about the activity, while the homework seemed just to consist of mindless repetition. The teacher saw that I was troubled by something and said, 'I can see what concerns you here.' Feeling relieved I waited for a possible explanation – perhaps a cover teacher had misunderstood the work, there was an emergency, maybe it was a joke. 'Yes,' she said, 'I know what you are thinking – those Hodder books really are out of date. Don't worry, we are buying some new ones!' She seemed surprised by my stunned silence. This school believed they were delivering on Assessment for Learning when clearly they had only the vaguest idea – dangerous indeed.

So beware thinking that you are an ace with Assessment for Learning merely because you are using the terminology. An amazing teacher needs to keep the focus on what the students are learning, how they are becoming more independent and how the objectives can be measured. We should always try to evaluate the success of the lesson against the objectives and intended learning. An amazing teacher also knows that amazing lessons are rarely silent ones – students often learn best when they are actively discussing and enquiring, not sitting like silent automatons!

- **Teach students how marks are awarded and the characteristics of a good piece of work**

  This is really important in helping students to become independent and understanding how to attain success. Show students examination criteria; rephrase it into student friendly language if necessary. Discuss and examine various samples of work. Tease out what makes some work effective and others not. Demonstrate how to mark a piece of work for themselves and teach students how to phrase what is working well and what could be made even better. Imagine sitting an examination yourself and not being told what you need to do to make sure you pass! As a learning expert the first thing you would want to do is to find out the success criteria.

Unfortunately when I speak to students in many lessons across the country and I ask them what they need to do to be successful in the piece of work they are completing, they are unclear, unable or just plain inaccurate. Teaching students how marks are arrived at demystifies the process and empowers the students as they realise there are no secrets – they can find out what they need to do to become successful and then do it! This is as true for teaching students the skill of gymnastics or how to design and produce a piece of work for textiles or how to write an essay – we forget it at our peril.

- **Teach students how to assess each others' work**

In one school I was conducting a friendly 'before inspection review'. Observing one class, the teacher asked me for my opinion. The students were completing a written commentary and she said she was either going to get them to self-assess their work or peer-assess it, and asked which I thought she should do. I asked her whether they had done either of these before and if the class had been trained in looking at each others' work. It transpired that they hadn't but this thought hadn't occurred to her. She was ready to let them loose correcting and commenting on each others' work without any training whatsoever. Obviously she knew that self- and peer-assessment were seen by inspectors as good things to be doing, rather like eating vegetables, but hadn't thought about how it needed to be managed and what the point was. If peer- and self-assessment are to have any real value, students need to be taught how to appropriately, fairly, tactfully and helpfully comment on each others' work. Above all they need careful training (which takes time and planning) with exemplar pieces that are carefully discussed as a class well before they are less loose on their classmates' work.

I have lost count of the times I have observed lessons and have been told that I am going to see some peer- or self-assessment and it ends up being a perfunctory 'swop books and look at your partner's work' which adds nothing to the learning and understanding of either party.

There are cautionary tales too if it is mishandled. I recall running some training in a primary school about the merits of peer-assessment and one teacher got very cross and said that peer-assessment had ruined her daughter's experience of GCSE Art. Upon closer examination it transpired that the teacher had asked students to comment on each others' work (without guidance or a marks scheme) and her daughter had been given some abusive and hurtful personal comments about herself as well as her work. Obviously the fault here is not the concept of peer-assessment, but the very real dangers of not introducing it to students in a supportive classroom environment so that constructive criticism remains just that – helpful and focused on the success criteria. Although these might seem extreme examples, this is by no means rare. All too often as an experienced subject practitioner it can seem blindingly obvious to us what makes a piece of work effective and what improvements are necessary, but we have to remember our students don't possess those skills unless we teach them.

Hold fire on the red pens too: you want parents to know which comments are yours and which are the result of peer- and self-assessment, otherwise you will get a critical phone call that accuses you of poor spelling! Encourage students to use a pencil or green pen and make sure you build in plenty of time for them to discuss the feedback with their partner. It is also a good idea to make your marking policy clear in the front of exercise books – showing parents, students and others what different colour pens mean and how pieces of work are marked. For example, notes that have been copied from the board may only receive a tick – if that – while extended pieces of work will have more detailed helpful comments with accompanying targets.

Thinking point

Consider your lessons over the last fortnight – it might help to have your planner with you. Think about your lessons and answer the following questions:

- Do I give students the opportunity to be involved in the assessment process? For example, do we discuss as a class what will make a piece of work good and draw up an agreed success criteria?
- Do I give students regular opportunities to have a focused discussion about their work with a partner and occasionally with me?
- Do I make sufficient time in lessons for students to review their work?
- Are students familiar with discussing success criteria and exemplar work?
- Is the climate in my classroom such that students feel confident and supported discussing their work with a partner or displaying it to their classmates?
- Are students clear about the strengths of their work and its weaknesses?

♦ Do students have personal targets that offer clear guidance about what they need to do to improve their work?

♦ Have they been involved in setting their personal targets?

There are various ways to get students more actively involved in reflecting on their own and their partner's work. Consider active ways such as:

♦ Using a pink highlighter for students to identify the part of the work they are 'tickled pink' by. This is a way of showing the section of the work that best meets the criteria. Using a green highlighter, get students to highlight a short piece of the text that has 'green shoots' for improvement. Remember, so that students don't run wild with highlighter pens, to get them to write in pencil next to the highlighted section what makes it effective or exactly how it could be improved. This can be a really focused way of getting students to look at their partner's work. It can also be surprisingly successful for identifying areas of improvement yourself.

♦ Asking students at the end of lessons to write down strengths and areas to improve on sticky notes.

♦ Getting students to write a summary statement detailing the advice their partner has given them. This may also help the student to internalise the advice.

- **Give students time to work and rework it**

There's little point spending hours marking students' work just to give it back very quickly then rushing on to the next topic. In order for students to fully benefit from your comments, ensure that you give them time either at the start of a lesson or near the end to actively respond to and act on your comments. After all, your marking comments won't be effective if you are having to make the same ones all term. Consider using examples of their responses as starter activities and make sure your class knows that you expect feedback on their work to be a two-way process.

Teachers very often feel they have not got time to revisit a topic or to allow students to take time to reflect on their work. However it is well worth setting aside fifteen minutes at the start of next lesson to do this. Not only will it save you some lesson planning, but you are reinforcing the fact that you expect students to value and to act upon what you have written. You need to ensure they get into the habit of doing this, at first under your eagle eye, so your comments start having a real impact. Make sure you give them specific issues to improve on – perhaps they have to try another Maths problem, improve an opening paragraph or use new vocabulary in several sentences. Whatever it is make sure that it is active and demands a response.

- **Review the learning that has been done in the lesson**

Remember, effective assessment isn't just about marking; it is about seeing how much students know and understand – and there are many more immediate ways of doing this. At the start of a lesson, it is a good idea to get a snapshot of the confidence level of the whole class. Traffic lights, five fingers on a hand or a simple thumbs up or down are all helpful indicators and can give you quick confirmation as to the amount of progress made. It can be sometimes more effective to do this because it gives you a snapshot of the whole class, rather than just asking a few individuals.

So remember, focus on the quality of assessment and how it can help students, rather than just spending hours correcting every last mistake.

Make your marking matter

The effectiveness of all of the advice above depends upon the quality of the feedback given.

So what characterises good quality feedback?

Good-quality feedback has several key qualities. It is specific to the learning objectives. We have already discussed the need to be really clear about what students are learning and the need to focus on the intended objective, rather than simply naming the task. Recently I watched a lovely Year 8 French class. The students were busily engaged with their work and, looking at the board, I tried to discover what they were learning. The objective stated: 'To learn how to write a leaflet about your school'. And there was bullet-pointed guidance about what to include, such as information about lessons, details about teachers, clubs, activities and school dinners.

When I walked around the class the students were happy to show me their colourful and well-designed leaflets. They were all enjoying the work and when I asked them what they needed to do to make a really good leaflet they invariably told me they had to: make it colourful, have good pictures and include all the information on the list.

I spoke to the teacher about the lesson and asked her why they were making leaflets and what she wanted them to learn from the task. Her answers were completely different: she wanted them to use two different tenses, write in sentences and use new vocabulary. Nowhere was this communicated to the students on the board or verbally; they were concentrating on entirely the wrong things.

I did not see the result of the teacher's feedback to the students, but I imagine one of two things happened. Either she would have focused the comments on her own criteria (which she had not communicated with the students) which would mean there was a strong likelihood that many of the students' work would have failed to meet the objective, or she would mark it without reference to the learning – merely focusing on layout, design and other incidentals. While the students might be more successful and motivated by such comments, since none of these were related to improving their French skills in the way she intended it is likely that the learning gains would be slim at best. So before we provide comments we need to be sure that we have provided clear learning objectives, that the students understand what they need to do to be successful – and our feedback or marking directly address these criteria. It is simple really, but it surprises me how often we get it wrong.

Feedback should also provide evidence of where the students are now. The best comments acknowledge with clear statements what the student has done to meet the criteria. These should be related to the learning objective and be positive in tone. For example: 'Well done Ian. You have used exciting description at the start of your story and interested the reader by asking a question.' Here the comment starts with praise, which is motivating and gives a clear comment about some precise things that Ian has achieved. It is very important that this should be followed up with any next steps. What would make Ian's work better? What precise skills does he need to improve? This should be written in a way that remains motivating – but by being precise makes future success achievable and manageable.

It is often the case that there are many things the students could and perhaps should do to improve their work; however giving too many pieces of advice can be very demotivating. How would you feel if you received the following comment: 'Ian, you need to try to make the story more exciting and develop the characters. Also think about how you describe the setting and work on the organisation of your work more.' Here, poor Ian is being asked to do too many things and the guidance isn't specific enough. How should he make the story more exciting? What does he have to do to develop the characters more? He also needs to 'think' about how he describes the setting, and 'work on the organisation of your work' sounds phrased more for a senior manager than giving a student clear advice. If you were Ian what would you do with this? I'd throw down my pen in despair, wouldn't you?

When writing a comment we need to bear in mind the need to be specific, clear and focused on the one or two things at most that would really improve the work and are a manageable next step for the student.

Thinking point

- How could the advice to Ian have been phrased better?

- Have a look at your own marking. What is the balance of comments like? Do you encourage students? Are you clear about what they have done well and is it equally clear what their next steps should be?

- Have a look at your students' books. Do they actually follow your advice? Do you give them time to go back over their work?

Interesting thought

Students interviewed about effective teachers' comments mention that they like the use of their name. Apparently it makes them feel that the comment is more personal, directed and that the teacher really knows them. So keep this in mind – but watch out when marking late at night – calling Simon, Samantha could have a very different effect!

Helping students to 'close the gap'

Make it very clear what you require students to do to improve their work. Be specific, such as: 'When you describe the characters add some physical description and use at least two interesting verbs to describe their actions.' Sometimes phrasing next steps as questions can be effective: 'What sort of atmosphere are you trying to create with the wood? What three words could you use to describe the wood to create this?' You will get a better response from students and help them make better progress if you are precise in your guidance.

It is also important to allow time not only for students to respond to the comment but for you to check what they have done. Some students I speak to don't respond to the teacher's comment because they don't know what it means. Make sure this is evident to students and discuss it with them if they have not followed up on it. The books of students in an amazing teacher's class don't have the same comments written in them lesson after lesson; the students make progress and therefore the marking comments show progress too – they address the *next* stages.

Students' comments on teachers' marking can be very insightful:

- 'Teachers expect you to know what they mean in comments' (but they don't explain them or check you know what they mean!).
- 'It would be better if teachers told me how I could improve my work.'
- 'If I get a "good", I don't usually know what I am doing well or what I need to improve.'
- 'My marks are always the same – I never know what I need to do to improve.'

There are two important points to draw from this. Students' perception of marking is crucial. Here the assumption is made that students automatically understand what you mean in your comments. This may be true, but it is important to periodically check this by discussing some of your comments with the students. Find out what they think they mean and how they intend to act on them. Be careful about giving bland positive comments, such as 'good'; students do need to know what exactly you like about their work and specific points help here.

Thinking point

The types of comments you make are very important. Have a look at the following remarks that I have found in students' books. Select two that you think are effective and another two that are poor.

1. You have got the general idea, Michelle, but the ending of the essay is very muddled.

2. A well-structured essay. Can you include another rhetorical device?

3. You have a made an error here with your working Ben (points to specific area). Have another go at this calculation remembering that the value of *x* is 15.

4. A lovely piece of personal writing – your granny sounds great!

5. Your work is far too disorganised! You do not even reach a final conclusion!

6. Why haven't you set this out properly?

7. A good story, I enjoyed it. Can you try to include another rhetorical device?

8. This is too messy! What happened to that good pen you were using last time?

9. You've not done this correctly! We went through the 3 stages in class!

Bear in mind the tone of your comments. Some of these – particularly some of those with the exclamation marks – sound downright angry. It can be incredibly frustrating marking books when students don't seem to have listened to a single word you have said. Sometimes it seems as if they can't be bothered to be accurate or have failed to get the point of the task. Sometimes you feel that you need to unleash your bitterness – but what will this really achieve except a temporary release? If you feel that the work you are marking has been inadequately completed or the class has missed the point, then it is best to stop marking, save your spleen and address the issue in the next lesson. Make sure you teach the topic again but try a different approach. Ensure that your instructions are very clear, then give your students a limited amount of time to correct or improve their work before you attempt to mark it. Sometimes students don't try hard enough with their first attempts because they know the teacher will accept and correct substandard work. An amazing teacher trains students so that they know this is not the case.

'A lovely piece of personal writing – your granny sounds great!' This seemingly innocuous comment has caused great controversy in the training I have held. What do you make of it? Is it a reasonable comment? Did it end up in your list of 'good' or 'terrible' comments? Firstly, it is positive in tone, which is a good thing. It is from a piece of personal writing that was set in a Year 7 English lesson. We have to remember that students are people and they do have feelings!

Secondly, it gives some very general praise –'lovely'. But what is particularly 'lovely' about this work? Thirdly, it seeks to build a relationship with the student and makes a pleasant observation about granny which is appropriate after a personal piece of writing. However the difficulty in this remark is what is *not* said – it would be ideal as the start of a comment but it does nothing to move that student on with their written work. It needs to be more precise in what is being praised and why the written work is good. Sometimes in marking too many comments focus on building relationships between students and staff and making generally pleasant comments, rather than helping the students improve their skill. There is a need for balance. We do need to build relationships with students – but the focus must remain on improving their skills and competencies.

Sometimes you flick through a book and there are lots of comments like this one: 'You do sound like you had a good holiday! Shame about all the rain though!' or 'Your father sounds like he was unlucky – I hope the scars and the fence are mended soon' or 'Yes, my rabbit did that too. Kylie is a great name.' It goes on . . . Obviously we neglect the personal at our peril. In some subjects, particularly English, Humanities and PSHE, students will write about very emotional subjects. If a student writes about their parents' divorce or describes the demise of their favourite hamster Harry (who has been vacuumed up by their over-domesticated mother) then it would be cruel and insensitive not to acknowledge this. Starting a comment with, 'Can you add two more similes to describe the blood and gore that sprayed out of the vacuum cleaner?' would be inappropriate and it is better in such cases to start with a sympathetic personal remark (students like this). However it does need to end with a clear, formative comment that relates to the learning objectives and the student's success in meeting them. If we fail to do this then we have not helped the student develop their work; we have perhaps improved our relationship with them but this is all.

'This is too messy! What happened to that good pen you were using last time?' This came from a boy's book that I flicked through when I was observing a lesson. On the surface it appears to be an appropriate observation, and at one level it is; sometimes comments do need to relate to the upkeep and presentation skills of students' books. However every single comment in his book was about his handwriting and his blasted pen. What made matters worse was the student was actually doing some very good work – he could write in a range of styles, he had generally accurate punctuation and some cracking vocabulary. Not one of these strengths was commented on. There were also some clear areas to develop but these were not mentioned in the marking either. All the comments had a strongly disapproving tone and they appeared not to have made the slightest difference.

Obviously if you have concerns about an area of a student's work they do need addressing. However if you find yourself making the same comment more than once then your chosen approach – here a rebuke and an urge to get it better next time – are clearly not working. When I mentioned the boy to the teacher she said, 'Oh Robert . . . he's got awful handwriting!' Clearly after writing the same comment hundreds of times it had stuck – but when I mentioned that these were the *only* comments she had made she looked rightly mortified. One of the dangers in marking and the tight, hardworking schedule we have as teachers is that sometimes the opportunity to flick back a few pages and see what we have written last time is missed – sometimes with unfortunate consequences. Marking needs to be constructive criticism that motivates the student to improve.

Assessment practice: make students look and learn

One of the best lessons I have observed was with a young overseas teacher who started his lesson by returning a set of books. Oh good I thought, at least he's marked his books up to date. He then explained to the class that when he started marking their books he found they had made lots of careless errors. He demonstrated by showing one of the students' work on the overhead projector. He encouraged the class to discuss what was good about it (there was plenty) and the boy whose work it was beamed from ear to ear. He then asked the class to pick out the lapses and errors and as a class they discussed how parts of it should have been written. After ensuring that the class were clear about this, he said he would be giving their unmarked books back and they would have ten minutes to make their corrections; only then would he take in their work for marking.

This is a good way of addressing the problem – it shifts the onus onto the student. It keeps your marking load manageable and by making the students responsible for checking and completing their work thoroughly *before* it gets to you means that some errors will be eliminated and those that remain will be the result of genuine misunderstanding rather than carelessness. Bear in mind when you start on a set of books, if more than a minority of students miss the point or make frequent errors then it is very likely that it is your teaching of the subject that is at fault or a lack of clarity in instructions. Before letting loose with the red pen think about whether you need to teach the topic in a different way or make your expectations clearer.

One of the difficulties with marking is the fact that students are more than happy to let you do all of the work for them – in fact many of them prefer it that way. I was running a training session in a top-achieving girls' independent school and one teacher stood up and passionately declared that in French lessons her students were so careless about how they put the accents on their letters, even though she knew that they were quite capable of doing it. 'What can I do? I spend all my life making these tiresome corrections!' she cried.

I related an incident that had happened to me a few weeks before that I felt shed some light on the matter. I had been in a primary school and was particularly interested in watching the progress of one boy, Sam. His teacher spent a great deal of time teaching the whole class about writing in sentences and I observed him using punctuation in a careful and deliberate way in the tasks. It seemed he had cracked it. I was taken aback in the next week to notice that his writing had reverted to a stream of consciousness without a comma or full stop in sight. I decided it was time for a little reminder and I started explaining the rules again. I was interrupted by Sam saying: 'Yes, yes, I know all that.' In response to my surprise as to why he was neglecting to use any punctuation he looked at me knowingly and said: 'You know it doesn't matter – because if I don't put any in Miss will do it for me!'

Of course we need to make appropriate corrections and that is the point of effective marking – we need to see what students can and can't do and give advice and corrections that close the gap accordingly. But we need to be careful that we don't create a dependency that simply invites the lazy (or should that be astute?) student to take advantage by letting Miss or Sir do all the work. An amazing teacher remembers that students need to be trained to stop and review their work *before* handing it in.

Thinking point

- Do I return marking promptly?
- Are my comments linked to the learning objectives in the lesson?
- If my comments are positive, do they give constructive, clear advice on next steps?
- For extended or important pieces of work are students given time to do something with the marking they receive?
- Are students clear about what they need to do in responding to my marking, and do their books demonstrate that this happens?

- If I notice several students made similar errors do I address this in the next lesson?

Reflection moment

What do I think my current strengths are in Assessment for Learning:

1.

2.

3.

How do I know? (Have I checked the books recently? Spoken to students?)

What areas do I need to develop further?

1.

2.

3.

What simple changes can I start next week?

1.

2.

3.

Section III

Achievement for All

Chapter 11

Everybody Counts

Every student who is taught by an outstanding teacher feels that *they* matter, that *they* are unique and that *their* needs are being catered for. Achieving this is no mean feat. It calls for a particularly positive attitude and interest in your students, as well as the awareness that we can all be prone to favour the student with the correct answers or winsome personality. Students expect and value scrupulous fairness and this is something that the outstanding teacher constantly strives to achieve.

In Section III we look at three different groups of students that can underachieve and provide some strategies and ideas to provoke thought and help you in the classroom. This chapter focuses on underachieving boys, chapter 12 on students with special educational needs and chapter 13 on Gifted and Talented students.

Dealing with Underachieving Boys

Boys' achievement has been a concern for the last twenty years or so. There was a time when teachers and politicians were concerned about girls and improving their attitudes towards more supposedly masculine subjects such as Maths and Science. However, in the majority of subjects girls are now outperforming boys. Many schools' results show that not only are countless boys not fulfilling their true potential, but their behaviour and attitude is a source of much anxiety. The group of students who are nationally the biggest underachievers are white, working-class boys. If you have ever taught a bottom set then you will be aware of the classroom management difficulties and motivational issues involved in dealing with a class that can be predominantly male and expecting not to succeed.

All this makes for pretty depressing reading and you may well be wondering, if it is a national problem, what can I possibly do with my underachieving boys in set 9X? Yes, it is a real national issue, but it is also true that some schools and some teachers are much more successful in ensuring that boys (and of course girls) achieve than others. It is by thinking about our own practice, by learning from those that succeed – and the boys themselves – that we can improve their attainment in our own classrooms.

Many of the issues connected with boys' underachievement are just as relevant to girls. Reassuringly, much of the latest research (my own included) suggests that there isn't anything amazingly different that needs to be done for boys. Much of what works is directly connected to good teaching, learning and classroom management by teachers. This should mean that improving achievement should be straightforward, but it does depend on consistent, effective and rigorous teaching. There are no easy solutions.

Who are the students that most lack attention? Who are the students that cause the most disruption in lessons? The majority of teachers who are asked these questions generally say 'boys' on both counts. However, observing behaviour in lessons often provides a very different picture. Yes, boys are generally much louder. When they are off task and disrupting the lesson it is usually much more noticeable. They are not quiet whisperers or doodlers; they horseplay and bellow. They do receive significantly more negative comments and rebukes from staff. However it is also true that girls can be off task just as frequently as boys, but in a quieter and more discreet manner. They are often chatting quietly or writing notes to each other in the backs of their books with one eye on the teacher. They are often not noticed when they are misbehaving and so escape criticism. This can lead to some boys feeling unfairly picked on, which can lead to an increasingly downward spiral in attitude, effort and achievement. So both boys and girls may lack attention in lessons but this is not always recognised and treated in an equitable way.

Are boys more astute critics of our teaching?

There are other reasons why boys and girls might achieve differently in the same classroom. Research on boys' achievement suggests that boys may actually be much more critical and astute about judging the quality of the teaching they receive, indicating that boys are less accepting of poor teaching than girls. This may have a ring of truth if you have ever observed a lesson that is not being taught in an engaging or interesting way, or perhaps had to deal with the aftermath of a badly supervised supply lesson. It is usually true that most of the students who have got on with the work and knuckled down, despite the poor teaching or boisterous atmosphere, tend to be girls rather than boys. They learn *despite* the quality of the teaching rather than because of it. Whatever the truth of this supposition, it does seem clear that what goes on in the lesson is particularly crucial in motivating boys.

So what practical strategies can you use in your classroom? Here are my top five effective teaching and learning strategies. Remember, they work for girls as well as boys and include plenty of common sense.

1. **Have high expectations – make sure you share these with students and parents**

   Too often in cases of underachievement too little is expected of students. When receiving really quite challenging targets for a class the first thought of some teachers often is: 'They will never achieve this. Ben a grade C? You must be joking.' It is easier to assume these targets are not achievable rather than to think, 'Right, Ben's currently on a grade E now. Why isn't he operating at a C level and what could be done about it?' Obviously there are sometimes good reasons such as poor attendance or illness, and these must be taken up with senior management, but all too often poor student attitude is mistaken for poor potential – leading to a vicious cycle of underachievement.

   Students clearly reflect their teachers' expectations of them and of course react accordingly. Whatever your doubts, you need to be relentlessly positive and tell your class you expect great things and exceptional progress, whatever their ability – and then follow this through by making sure your teaching helps them to achieve it. Listen to the way you speak to your students and ensure that you treat the D/E student like the potential C grade he should be. Focus on what they *should* be achieving and be clear about the skills they need to get there. Don't forget to communicate this positively to both students and parents. You will be impressed by the results that come from expecting more. In fact many parents can feel that teachers have 'written off' their child. If you make the effort to explain that they have potential, explain fully the scope of this, and take the time to contact them indicating this, then they are far more likely to be supportive and reinforce positive messages about putting in an appropriate amount of effort.

Recently I was invited into a school to teach some specialist revision sessions. I was asked to teach one particular class for two hours – an extended lesson. Two-hour lessons are not ideal particularly with borderline students (boys in particular can swiftly lose concentration) but after running my intensive session I was impressed. From a sluggish and 'can't really be bothered' start, they put their hands up, answered at length and came up with some pretty impressive work. I rewarded them with a great deal of verbal praise, and one boy came up to me at the end, abashed and slightly confused. 'Do you know what, Miss?' he commented, 'You're the first teacher who has said I'm any good at English – ever.' I let it sink in for a moment, and then showed him his work and talked about its strengths.

This young man of 15 or 16 was due to take his final examinations in a matter of days. He clearly was a student who had the potential to achieve his target grade (hence the special revision sessions with yours truly) but the damning fact remained that the few words of meaningful praise I had given him had not been given elsewhere, ever. If students are to achieve their potential they have to believe they can succeed, and this means the teacher telling them and acting towards them as if they really have the potential to succeed.

One of the tips I have learnt from teaching these sessions (and working in an all-boys' school) is to keep lessons tightly focused, make students feel they are achieving and praise them relentlessly for good work. There is no magic in this – nothing new, but expecting a lot from students is essential. Immediately when I meet a new group I tell them that their teachers (or track record) tell me there are some talented individuals in the class. This makes it very clear that I am expecting the best from them and that they really do have something to offer. With some classes it is even possible to detect a physical difference as students literally sit up, straighten their backs and pay attention. They are also keyed up to prove that the view you have of them is correct.

However, in schools or classes where boys are underachieving teachers simply do not tap into this aspiration. If fact, if you don't make all students feel they can achieve and make progress in each and every lesson, then the effects can be catastrophic. In my experience it is particularly important with boys, who thrive on praise and seem to need their delicate self-belief reinforcing every step of the way.

It is a very sad day when a visiting speaker sees more potential in a student than his teacher of several years – but it is by no means a rare occurrence. When I meet students, I don't know their reputation. I expect the best from them and communicate this to them straightaway. They respond, I praise them more then increase the challenges and demands within the lesson and then they really are succeeding! We can all do this: it is the key to building successful relationships with the individuals within our class and in securing achievement and lifelong success. But we have to remember that it starts with *us* – our mental attitude, our positive approach and most importantly our expectation and how that is communicated.

2. **Signal exactly why you are doing something. Why is it important? How does it fit into the bigger picture?**

Talking to boys who work well in lessons and who are making good progress they often comment upon the reasons why they are completing a piece of work and how it fits into the greater scheme of things. When speaking to a couple of lads in a low-ability GCSE group, who were working very diligently improving and adding to a piece of coursework, they explained their motivation simply by saying that they knew the piece of coursework was important (even knowing the percentages it was worth). They explained that the teacher had given them clear indications about what aspects they needed to improve – and thereby a carrot by indicating that they could improve their marks by up to a grade if they made the extra effort. There was a sense that even though they weren't the brightest students, they could still improve their work and make significant progress and were being helped to do so.

Conversely, students who are disaffected and unmotivated often mention that they 'can't see the point of doing . . . ' – often not understanding how the work relates to coursework or the examination. I have heard teachers say, and have probably said myself in desperation and frustration, 'But you *need* to work to get good GCSEs to get a good job.' This pseudo-threat seems to have little effect on boys' behaviour because, as one told me, 'That's ages away, Miss.' The carrot, it seems, is much more effective than the stick. So make sure your classes know the big picture: where they are going this term/year and how each lesson contributes towards the middle-term goals, whether that is a particularly important piece of homework, coursework, learning a skill or revising for a forthcoming test.

3. Show the class what 'good' looks like

This should be simple. Show the class exemplars of good pieces of work before they start the task. Sometimes breaking it into chunks – for example, showing the class several introductions to an essay – is a good idea rather than overwhelming them by looking at a fifteen-page essay in its entirety. Empower the class by getting them to identify what is effective about the work and what could be improved. Boys in particular have commented that they really wanted to see what something could look like before they start work. Make sure the class knows the success criteria for every piece of work; they are much better motivated if they know what is expected and feel more confident that success is within their reach. If you find that you are not doing this as much as you might then read over Section III on Assessment for Learning, which explores these techniques and their importance in greater depth.

4. Make the learning interactive and fun

Boys, like all of us, have limited attention spans. If our attention is strained by a dull or overlong activity then we divert it onto something more interesting, such as kicking Eric or texting our friends. Simple changes to the way a task is set out can ensure that students are more motivated, engaged and interested. So, for example, instead of giving the whole class twenty questions to answer on a worksheet (knowing that some will answer them all, and a few will start one or two but then drift off) divide the task up, put students into groups or pairs and give them particular responsibility for a certain number of questions, explaining that they will be the particular experts on those questions. Giving students responsibility for specific outcomes and breaking down tasks into manageable and interactive chunks makes learning much more effective and reduces the chance that they 'won't bother' to complete it.

Develop and experiment with a range of interactive teaching techniques that demand that students get involved and get active. Passive listening does not lead to long-term retention and can be boring, leading to inevitable off-task behaviour.

5. Include plenty of praise

Think about how you phrase things and how often you praise. Do you suggest things in a positive manner using terms such as 'challenge' or instead nag at students about 'work' with the threat of 'detentions'? It can be hard to speak more positively, but words of praise should be used frequently. Think about how you introduce tasks. For example, a starter activity could be employed whereby students have to find five quotations about Lennie in *Of Mice and Men*. How would you instruct the class? You could make it sound like hard work – or quick, fun, dynamic and by using terms such as 'quiz', 'who can do this?' or 'off you go!' If we do this learning becomes fun and importantly it gives you the opportunity to offer meaningful praise.

Remember every student wants to feel liked and that their teacher thinks that they are doing well. In many lessons the ratio of praise to criticism is far too low. Research shows that in some classes students are told off seven times or more against every good comment. And you've guessed it: it's the boys who receive much less praise and lots more criticism. It can be easy to become a nag; instead comment on the behaviour you would like to see. Instead of picking on those students who aren't behaving, praise those who are. Make a conscious effort to increase praise fivefold in your lessons and you will be surprised by the energy and efforts your students, particularly the boys, will show.

Creating the right ethos

An amazing teacher aims to have the sort of atmosphere in the classroom whereby all students feel comfortable about receiving praise and the classroom climate is supportive of this. In one amazing teacher's classroom, after one student had made a great comment and the teacher paused for breath before thinking what to say about such a startlingly good answer, the room was roused by a spontaneous round of applause by the class. This was a truly wonderful thing to observe. The student's classmates were genuinely impressed by his contribution and showed this in a lovely way. As you can imagine, this was a very good school that celebrated achievement by all students and had a very positive ethos.

The right ethos is created by the way the teacher shows respect and admiration for her students. It is created by the values she demonstrates and by the way the students are encouraged to respect and value each other across a school, in a culture where achievement is valued. Students at this school felt comfortable praising each other and being praised in turn. In some schools an unpleasant 'anti-learning' culture dominates and it can be difficult to develop a positive learning ethos if students are jeered at for answering or if they are called 'boffin' by their peers. This is a sign that something is very wrong in the school, and it makes creating the right culture in your classroom harder but not impossible. If students are resistant to praise this does not mean that you shouldn't give it. It may mean that initially praise is given individually at the end of the lesson or to small groups of students, but ultimately we must strive to have classrooms where it happens readily and openly.

Remember that *all* students secretly like and want to be praised. One strategy for breaking the perception that some boys feel it is 'not cool' to be praised or to be seen as working hard is to place students into groups for some of the work and then praise and reward the groups before moving on to individuals. The effective use of praise can really transform the work ethic and atmosphere in a classroom, so make it a top priority in your lessons.

Thinking point

- Are you clear about what the predicted grades and targets are for all students in your class?
- Are you sure these are challenging enough? What do you do in your behaviour and with the lessons you design to help boys feel they can achieve?
- Be brave – ask a friend to observe you with a specific focus, such as how often you praise or the ratio of comments to boys and girls. Take on their feedback and plan any necessary actions or amendments.
- Make a note somewhere you can see when you are teaching – perhaps a code word – reminding you to praise boys (and girls too) more frequently. Observe the progress when this happens.
- Ask for honest or perhaps anonymous feedback on your lessons from the students. For example, give boys and girls different coloured sticky notes. End all lessons

once a fortnight with a question such as, 'How much did you join in and what could encourage you to join in more?' Ask students to stick their answers on the door as they leave. You will then be able to observe the different responses and reflect upon what is working well and what might be improved.

- Make sure you clearly signal *why* you are making students do something, *how* it will benefit them and *what* you are expecting by sharing the success criteria and/or showing an exemplar piece of work.

- Take time each week to give positive feedback to parents when things have gone well. A praise postcard or even better a phone call to parents will have a tremendous effect on students' motivation and relationship with you and their parents. It is really worth setting aside the thirty minutes or so a week that it will take to do this.

- Imagine an underachieving boy is a firm favourite of yours (of course you don't have favourites) and that he is really bright. How would you act towards him? Do it now!

- When setting work revise how you can describe it: go for 'quiz', 'challenge' or 'adventure'. Call the learning 'fun' (in a convincing way) and be prepared for interest and productivity levels to rise.

- Frequent small rewards (praise, stickers, merit marks, etc.) and a positive, competitive feel to tasks can awaken some lethargic boys and help them to take an interest in the lesson.

Chapter 12

Ensuring the Progress of SEN Students

All students have particular needs, however it is crucially important to be alert to students who have special educational needs to ensure that you know what these are, what you can do to help the student make good progress and to ensure that you address these in lessons and any homework you set.

This is not the place to give details on specific special needs because sometimes over-generalisation can be misleading. Further information about individual students and their particular needs should be sought from the special educational needs coordinator (SENCO) or inclusion manager at your school. This is particularly important because they will provide you with the precise information you require. Most students with statements will have an Individual Education Plan (IEP) and these will include specific targets for the student as well as detailing information about their needs and what help must be given to them. There will also be students at School Action and School Action Plus and you will need to make sure you also accommodate their needs in your lessons.

It is vital to be clued up on all available information relating to a student's needs. You need to ensure this is ready to hand because this is of obvious importance in planning lessons that are appropriate to the student's needs. These details should also be made available to others who are supporting the student such as learning support assistants.

Lessons should be planned so that *all* students whatever their ability and needs can make suitable progress. A PE teacher recently said to me on a training course: 'I can never teach an outstanding lesson with my particular PE classes because I've got the weak swimmers and they can never make really *good progress*.' This is a misconception. While the weak swimmers are never going to be award-winning swimmers, an outstanding teacher tries to ensure that they all make outstanding progress. Progress is about measuring where a students is now and reviewing how far the lesson or series of lessons has moved them on.

One of the dangers with special educational needs (SEN) students is expecting too little of them. We should still set challenging lessons (as we would for any student) but the lesson needs to be appropriate to their starting point. There is a balance to be struck of course, but all students of all abilities need appropriate challenge and encouragement to become independent learners.

There are some key things that you can do as a teacher to help students make appropriate progress and to ensure that the learning environment is conducive to this. Some of the following have been successful; however remember that students are individuals and what may work well with one student might not be so successful with others.

- Be clear and consistent in your instructions.

- Be careful not to give too many instructions at once. Sometimes reinforcing verbal instructions with words on the board or other visual clues (such as cue cards) will help.

- Be prepared to repeat instructions and ask students to repeat instructions back to check their understanding.

- Make sure students understand not only what they are required to do but what success for this piece of work looks like. It is important to break down success criteria into very small steps.

- It is often a good idea to show students an exemplar piece of work to start them off or use writing frames and other scaffolding devices. Bear in mind that a blank piece of paper can be very daunting, so asking students to rework or improve a piece of less effective work is a good way in.

- Use discussion and talk first. Students who have difficulty expressing their ideas on paper often benefit from structured opportunities to discuss and plan their work verbally before writing.

- Teach planning as an explicit skill. Mini-whiteboards, sticky notes, diagrams and plans can provide effective strategies for helping students to sequence and order their thoughts. It is also important for students to know that it is fine to rethink and reorder their original ideas. Teaching planning skills shows students that they don't have to get it right first time and that work is often better if it is given some thought and consideration.

- Check the reading level of the material you are giving to students is within their grasp. This does not mean 'dumbing down' the work but it may mean that you need to be explicit about some of the vocabulary (it is often good practice to demonstrate and get students involved in looking up new words in a dictionary). Be aware that some students may struggle with a text and support them accordingly (e.g. giving them the opportunity to pre-read the text).

- Make sure students can see the board and that the environment helps them to focus rather than providing a distraction. Think carefully about seating arrangements and acoustics.

- Consider what work you set – some students really struggle with taking notes and recording information. This does not mean that you shouldn't set such work, but provide guidance on how best to do this. Consider whether it is necessary for students to copy out an overlong learning objective when this laborious act may switch them off right at the start of the lesson.

- It is important to make learning achievable in bite-size chunks so that it is clear what the student is doing and it isn't going to overwhelm them. Sometimes using visual information or breaking down tasks helps to keep students motivated and on task.

- Some students will have low self-esteem and feel they are failing in the school system. Meaningful praise, good relationships and focused tasks that show incremental learning are a good way of helping students to feel good about themselves and their learning. Some students will not read what you have written in their book, so make sure you give sufficient verbal praise, talk over their written work with them – showing them what you have enjoyed about the work – and set very clear, achievable guidance for improvements. It is also important to allow some classroom time for these improvements to be made.

- ICT can be a real benefit in encouraging students to write at length, to investigate and take pride in their work.

- Think carefully about when and how you set homework in lessons. Rushing to set homework in the last fifty seconds is poor practice anyway, but will cause real difficulties for many SEN students. Take time to explain homework carefully and avoid them having to copy out a range of complicated instructions from the board.

- Statements are reviewed regularly and you will be expected to make useful comments about the student's progress in relation to their targets. Do keep dialogue between staff frequent and useful. Finding out which colleagues are having particular successes, feeding back information to the form tutor or asking for further guidance from the SENCO or inclusion manager are all key in addressing a student's needs and helping them to make good progress in your subject. Don't forget communication with the family – ensure that they are informed about what is working well and that you share successes with them. Many families are keen to know what they can do to support their student; if they are, be very precise about what would help and give sufficient guidance about how this should be done.

The role of learning support assistants

In some of your lessons you will have learning support assistants (LSAs). It is *your* job to make sure that this partnership is a success and that the LSA is clear about the work that is being set and what needs to be achieved. In addition you will also want to receive feedback from the LSA about the lesson: How did the student manage? What was successful? What do they still need to work on? What was too challenging? What was too easy? How suitable were the resources?

I have seen many first-hand examples of LSAs adding an enormous amount of value to lessons, ensuring that students' needs are met and enabling them to fully engage and make progress in the lesson. This only happens when they are very clear about what the student is expected to achieve and if they understand the work themselves. In one excellent lesson I observed, at the end of the session the LSA gave the teacher some very specific comments about what the student had achieved and what was still needed. It was only a short exchange but it meant the teacher was clear about progress and could tailor the next lesson accordingly. The teacher's interaction with the LSA also revealed that they were very much valued in the classroom and that teacher and assistant alike were working together as a team. In other instances LSAs will be helping groups of students with a specific piece of work. Make sure your assistant is very clear about what help you expect them to offer, how much guidance they should be giving to students and the success criteria for a piece of work.

When partnerships between teacher and LSA are less effective this is usually because of poor communication or unclear expectations. On occasion, I have observed an LSA ask a student to focus upon something in their work that wasn't of key importance and he was told 'not to worry' about something else that was integral to the success of the work. Upon further investigation it transpired that the LSA had not been given a proper briefing, and neither the scheme of work, example work or marking policy had been explained to her. The progress and success of all students remains the responsibility of the classroom teacher; it is important therefore to work well with your LSA to ensure that all students develop and reach their potential.

All students, regardless of ability, should make good progress in lessons and should feel appropriately challenged by the work set. Don't fall into the trap of not expecting enough from SEN students. Students need to feel that they are in a supportive atmosphere so they can try to push themselves. Students will only be willing to take risks if you show that you believe in them, and if you make the work interesting, engaging, challenging but ultimately achievable.

Thinking point

- Am I clear about which students have special educational needs and what I need to do to help them achieve?
- Are these students making good progress in my lessons? Do they enjoy them? Do they participate and feel valued? How do I know?
- Do I feel I have sufficient expertise with students' particular needs? Do I need to observe a teacher who is particularly successful in teaching this student? Do I need further specialist training? Is there further advice or resources the school SENCO could give me?
- How well do I work with my LSAs? Do we work effectively as a team? Do I request and listen to feedback from them? Do I ask for feedback and do I give them sufficient information so they can make a difference to that student's progress?
- Am I aware of what barriers there are to learning? Am I addressing these?

- Look again at the work of one of your students over two or three months. Can you see sufficient progress in their work?

Chapter 13

Teaching Gifted and Talented Students

> Set challenges for students. Students may complete work to a decent standard, but will be capable of much more. I know I enjoyed rising to the challenge.
>
> Dan Coventry, Gifted and Talented student

Teaching Gifted and Talented students can be a great joy. Sharing your enthusiasm for quadratic equations, Henry VIII or the subtleties of Shakespeare's language with a talented and enquiring class can remind you of why you went into teaching in the first place. We need to remember that having a dialogue with really talented students can be a beneficial learning experience for the teacher as well as the student. Even if you have taught a topic twenty times before, the ability of some students to make you think about it completely differently can take your breath away.

However, teaching Gifted and Talented students is certainly one area that for many teachers requires improvement before they can be considered amazing. It is not always a positive experience for the teacher or the highly intelligent student, and there are a few key reasons behind this. It is an unfortunate truth that, in many schools across Britain, Gifted and Talented students receive a tough deal because their potential is not always realised by teachers and the teaching does not push, challenge or inspire them to reach their maximum.

Many teachers are surprised by this, but the facts in some classrooms paint a worrying picture. I am going to ask you to think of a classroom. It is a top set, say an English lesson. I want you to imagine the cleverest student in that class. Got it? Good. What do they look like? How do they act? Where do they sit in the classroom? How do they interact with the teacher and the rest of the class? What does their book look like? What is their attitude towards homework? You should have a picture in your mind. Great. Now tell me about it.

The response I most often get is that the most able student is a very hardworking, diligent, neat-looking girl! Always motivated, one of the first to hand in work, sitting at the front of the classroom, often next to an equally diligent friend. I'll admit there are plenty of very able students who meet these criteria – in fact I meet plenty of them in top sets when I visit schools. In fact they dominate – sometimes they truly are the most Gifted and Talented student in the class. Sometimes yes, but very often the *really* gifted students are overlooked.

It is important to explode the myths regarding the most able, gifted or however you wish to describe these students. Because without an amazing teacher, very many of them underachieve and fail to meet their potential. There are some key reasons behind this fact.

1. Identification

Many teachers believe they can easily spot gifted students, and they fill classes with biddable, neat, well-behaved and often very 'good' (in both senses of the word) students. Many of the potentially brightest students in our schools fail to achieve because they are simply not perceived as being gifted. Sadly we label and judge students very quickly and those that challenge the rules, look a little scruffy or choose to subvert a task to their own choosing can be seen as awkward and not gifted at all.

In many schools teachers confuse compliance and competence for giftedness. If you are a middle-class, female student you are much more likely to be put in a top set than perhaps a more talented boy who is known for being disruptive. Some of the most amazingly talented students are those that can be unlikeable or just plain troublemakers. If they come from a background where not much is expected of them and parental influence or interest is lacking they will almost certainly fail to achieve. That is unless the amazing teacher spots their potential and harnesses this in lessons so that they can shine.

While I am not saying that all disruptive students are gifted (sometimes they are just naughty!) it is often true that very clever students have character traits that you might not expect. They get bored very easily and can, if they feel that they are not being challenged appropriately, become lazy, disaffected and occasionally very disruptive.

Just because your school has setting arrangements don't feel that this does the job of identifying the students for you. It is all too common to hear teachers talk about students 'not deserving a place in the top set' (although they are actually clever enough) because of their poor behaviour. Is it any more likely they will behave well if they are placed in a set that is clearly working at an insultingly low rate? I think not.

Very gifted students can get themselves into enormous trouble. If they are not motivated and engaged by lessons some students may even go so far as getting themselves excluded or expelled from school. Very bright students are much less tolerant of bad teaching than their less able counterparts. They can be a nightmare to deal with because they can be sharp-tongued enough to floor you with a caustic comment! They can expose your shortcomings and any gaps in your knowledge to the rest of your class in a way that a more obviously unruly but less intelligent student has no chance of ever doing.

Unfortunately in my first year of teaching I had this experience. There was a boy in my Year 9 class, let's call him Leigh. He was disruptive, rude and obnoxious. His book was a mess and he made it very clear that he often found the work 'dull' at best. I was teaching a difficult topic for the very first time and if on occasion I double-checked something or hesitated he and a few of his cronies mocked me. Leigh, it appeared, was a very unpleasant boy, who rarely handed in homework and had the most atrocious, messy handwriting ever seen. He would stroll in late and regard the lesson with ill-concealed disdain through half-closed lids. When I was giving him my assessment level at the end of the year, I naturally thought he was nothing better than a middle to low average. I remember being quite amazed as well as dismayed when the results of his module came through and he had got the top grade in the year. His poor behaviour, attitude and disagreeable habits meant that I had been oblivious to his obvious ability, and his scornful attitude meant I had not worked hard enough to praise, encourage or push him.

In my first year of teaching I was painfully aware of my lack of teaching expertise and knowledge in some areas of the curriculum and so had allowed myself to react sharply to a student who enjoyed exposing these gaps. Perhaps if I had noticed and harnessed this ability earlier he would have felt more encouraged and challenged. I like to think I now have the experience and confidence to have played it a little differently, but it was an important lesson in judging students and made me realise that poor behaviour sometimes stems from a lack of challenge in the work set – as well as a hostile and immature teenage mentality.

2. Keep an open mind – let them impress you

When you are given your classes, or when you meet students for the first time, try to keep an open mind. Students are too often branded as being clever, or not, on the personal and sometimes biased view of a single teacher. I am sure we have all got examples of when a personality clash or closed mind judged us before we had really the chance to make our mark – don't let this happen to you. An amazing teacher needs to constantly strive to keep an open mind and give students of all abilities the opportunity to impress us with their achievements. An Advanced Skills Teacher Michelle Syned shares a tip: 'Give a choice of tasks, questions or assessments; there is very little to complain about if they've chosen the activity!'

It also helps if we remember that very able students aren't always conformists – far from it! Think of the world's greatest artists, musicians, scientists, writers . . . what often makes them exceptional is the fact that they broke the rules and were not afraid to experiment in their search for answers. Obviously in school there are certain parameters: perhaps an assessment needs to be completed to certain specifications or there needs to be a specific outcome. If this is the case then certainly you shouldn't abandon the guidelines in the quest for greater creativity or increased freedom. But it does mean making the reason behind them very clear to students. Very often there are choices, so why not free up the reins at little and let students make a preference? If you are teaching students of middle ability you might need to keep things very tight with careful and constant guidance to keep them all on track. But be careful this attitude doesn't seep in when it isn't needed; giving the brightest students a very short leash may really curtail their enthusiasm and opportunity to shine. Treat all students in an adult way by explaining what success criteria the work needs to fulfil, but promote discussion of viable options in the way it might be completed.

3. Have high expectations

It is so true that teacher expectation is one of the most important things in determining student success. Expect the best of all of your students. Be positive and try to inspire them whenever and wherever you can. The odd word of encouragement – 'I've just started marking your essay, James, and it is really good' – while they are standing in the dinner queue can have a magic effect. Go on, try it!

We are guilty of making too many assumptions too quickly about individuals and their abilities. Try to resist this and make sure you give all students every opportunity to show you what they can really do. Be diligent about setting appropriate work and in collecting and marking it thoroughly. Students easily switch off if they feel you have not responded appropriately or quickly enough to their work.

Dan Coventry, now a university student, remembers a poor experience at a school:

> I had completed a series of comprehension booklets which were ordered by colour. Once I had finished the hardest books (brown) I thought my teacher would be impressed. In fact, she relegated me to the most basic level and accused me of cheating. This incident caused me to hide my intelligence . . . this example may demonstrate one of the reasons behind the unwillingness of a student to display their intellect, as they wonder: 'What difference will it actually make?'

Students can easily turn off if they feel the teacher is not interested in their efforts or as in Dan's case they are slighted and not given the necessary praise. Not having a clear idea of a student's potential means that work can be set at an insultingly low level and as Dan's comment indicates disaffection and rebellion can set in with even the brightest student.

Underachieving but gifted students often can be the biggest slackers when it comes to handing in homework – but persevere. Sometimes it is only when you push the issue that you will actually see what your students are capable of. It was only when I'd wrestled an exquisitely written and beautifully crafted story from a scruffy looking rebel that I began to realise that maybe I was dealing with an incredibly talented individual . . .

4. You don't always have to be the expert!

> My idea of an outstanding lesson is one in which, to all intents and purposes, the students feel as though they are teaching themselves and each other through their own active engagement in the lesson. In the very best

lessons I have seen, the teacher moves from director to facilitator, creating the conditions through which students can take responsibility for their own learning and learn with – and through – one another. This is very challenging – planning is all – but it is the most exciting teaching to observe when it is done well.

Rick Holroyd, head teacher, Langtree School ”

The comment above provokes several thoughts. In an amazing teacher's lessons, the focus is clearly on the students – what are they learning, how are they achieving, how the lesson is benefiting them. It is not a circus where the teacher demonstrates their 'tricks' or knowledge for the entertainment of the students. The students need to be at the centre of the learning. It is obvious that this focus depends upon clear and careful lesson planning by the teacher, but it also depends upon an understanding that for a lesson to be really successful the students need to be in the driving seat – empowered to learn and sometimes discovering things for themselves, rather than being spoon fed by an expert. For many teachers this can be unsettling – after all aren't we the expert? Isn't that why we are the teacher? This viewpoint can also lead to dull lessons in which teachers tell students, often in a very dry fashion, all they need to know – and then wonder why they don't retain any of these precious pearls of wisdom. This standpoint of teacher as expert can lead to real difficulties when teaching particularly Gifted and Talented students.

Many teachers believe they always have to be an authority and know the right answer. If you can manage to dispel this myth then you are well on the way to creating the right classroom culture to nurture every latent Einstein or budding Shakespeare. This does not mean that you don't need to do your homework or know your stuff. To gain students' respect and confidence you need to show them they have a teacher who is on top form, who knows their subject, has a passion for it and is willing to work hard to keep up with recent developments. But this doesn't mean you won't ever make the occasional mistake or forget something. What matters is how you deal with it.

Think about how you respond to students' questions and corrections. A friend of mine was given a detention at school for pointing out (probably with glee) that his teacher consistently made errors in mathematical problems. He was damned for 'thinking himself far too clever'. He was constantly told off for calling out and making corrections, instead of shutting up and listening to the teacher's answers (even if that meant ignoring her mistakes). He later read Maths at Oxford University. Think about the various tactics this teacher could have used to stretch this gifted student – and keep her dignity intact.

If you can encourage students to see that despite being highly successful you still might make careless mistakes or have areas of weakness, you teach them a valuable lesson. Also remember that for a student to have identified that you have given the wrong date for a battle or calculated something incorrectly then they are at the very least being alert and paying serious attention to what you are doing. It has been known for some teachers to throw in the occasional 'deliberate' mistake (or that's what they told me) as a tactic to encourage focused attention – as long as students don't retain the incorrect information.

Teaching students who have greater skills than you

It is a fact that you will teach students who are much more intelligent than you. Imagine how you would feel if you questioned a teacher's comment and were told: 'Don't interrupt me!' (which really means, 'Hey shut up, I'm the expert – pin back your ears and listen cretin!')? Or alternatively received recognition for making the teacher think about a subject in a totally different way? I recently ran a revision session in which one boy said something that I had not thought of before. He was quite right but nobody else had ever spotted it – not even me. I told him this, praised him a little and mentioned that nobody had thought of this before. He literally grew before my eyes – he straightened up, beamed and worked unbelievably hard for the rest of the day, swaggering as he strode into the next class claiming he'd loved the lesson and had learnt loads – powerful stuff indeed. He was motivated by the fact that I'd had the brass neck to admit he'd out-thought me. Don't be afraid of doing this: sometimes relishing the fact that you don't have all the answers is the right way to push and encourage your most able students. And hey, learning something new yourself is what makes teaching such an interesting and challenging job.

Thinking point

This month:

- Watch your class in another subject that gets lots of top grades. Are there any surprises? Do different students shine? How does the teacher push and challenge them? Do you do it as well? Watch and learn. Look at: task setting, use of questions, student involvement and how the work is made to push and challenge the students.

- Ask a colleague to observe you on how you challenge your class and individual members in it. Ask them to provide a constructive critique.

- Review the work you have set for all students. Did the Gifted and Talented get more of the same additional work to plough through, or was the work pitched at a challenging enough level the first time? What is the quality of their work like? As them how they felt about doing it. Do they get enough input into the lesson content and design?

- Ask your class for feedback about your lessons – either through sticky notes at the end of lesson, a survey, a written questionnaire or even as a small group interview. Ideally get a colleague to do this for you, as often students will tell you what they think you want to hear or you will listen selectively. Take on board their ideas. Make changes as necessary and evaluate these.

This week:

- Do I know who the school data suggests are the most able?

- Are these students performing well? Check out reasons for underperformance and eliminate them.

- Treat all students as if they are capable of the very best. Set the bar high.

- Investigate new and challenging teaching resources. Ask department members for teaching strategies that work well with very able students. Remember, everybody likes variety and resources must be tailored to the right ability.

- Contact parents and use the school reward system for those that have achieved exceptionally well. Often very able students are expected always to perform well and miss out on the rewards and praise that less able students often receive. Remember, all students thrive on praise – particularly if it is specific, targeted and genuine.

This lesson:

- Think about what work I am setting this week. Can I allow some choice? Can I get students involved in determining the success criteria or shaping the type of work needed?

- Tell my class they are 'very intelligent'. Tell them I am setting them something challenging because they have the ability. Look at their body language and motivation. Do you see an increase in effort? Say it like you mean it! Be genuine.

- Think about pushing students through extended questioning and asking them to back up their answers or build on someone else's. Are you taking them to the brink of their knowledge?

- Be very specific in the oral and written feedback you give students. Are the students very clear about what they need to do to improve their work and take it on to the next level? Consider showing them excellent exemplar work and discuss the characteristics that make it really good so they can do this in their own work.

- Look out for individuals. Who isn't joining in? Is anyone switched off? Keep alert for signs of underachievement and try to find out about any barriers and then re-engage the student.

- Celebrate success by giving verbal praise and using your school reward system.

Personalisation

I heartily dislike this term although it is a current buzzword in educational circles. First coined by a government minister, educationalists freely use this term although many seem very hazy about what it actually means. I once bet a friend that the best way to unhinge any conversation with an education expert is to ask what personalisation means – in simple terms in just one sentence. I have destabilised many an important meeting by doing this (try it yourself!). Nobody yet has been able to do it without saying, 'Well it isn't . . .'

My advice is to avoid meaningless educational jargon. Instead an amazing teacher should concentrate on the basics by focusing on the following areas:

- Check that no groups of students or individuals are underachieving in your lessons. I have mentioned three groups that frequently underachieve: white, working-class boys, SEN students and some Gifted and Talented students. Clearly there may be other students – perhaps in your school it is girls or English as an Additional Language (EAL) students. Be alert to any individuals who underachieve and take steps to deal with it.

- Finding and recognising underachievement can and should be done in a number of ways, such as checking school exam results against targets and RAISE online data analysis. However often this can be leaving things too late. We need to be constantly checking that students are on target, that motivation, work ethic and attendance is on track and participation levels in classrooms is good.

- Audit yourself from time to time. Who do you praise most? Who gets the most detentions? What groups of students are joining in the most? Who are the individuals who are stuck or sidelined in lessons?

- Don't just rely on your own views – we have our own blind spots and sometimes we miss the obvious. Ask a colleague to observe a lesson and give them a particular focus – listen to what they say! Ask students for their views but don't shoot the messenger and make sure that however you do it students feel they can speak honestly without worrying that it will tarnish your view of them.

- Seek good practice from experts within your own school and beyond. Sometimes doing some further reading or attending a quality training course can help you refocus your energies on areas that need improvement.

Remember, many of the suggestions for engaging and helping students to achieve are similar regardless of their ability or background. Getting the best out of *all* students means knowing them really well as individuals. Be clear about what they need to do to improve their current work and make sure the lessons you provide give them all the scope to achieve this. It is a combination of your high expectations, quality lesson planning and use of praise that has the power to transform the learning in your classroom from average to amazing.

Section IV

Solving Tricky Issues and Difficulties

Chapter 14

Body Language

The Power of Positivity

This chapter deals with how we respond to students but also how we present ourselves in the classroom and around the school. Even before we open our mouths we have created an impression on our students whether for good or otherwise. The amazing teacher is a master of using their body language to get across a particular message, create a particular atmosphere in the classroom or manage a difficult situation.

We will first look at the power of body language, and then what happens when we actually open our mouth. Giving a little thought to how we express ourselves can have magical effects in the classroom and promote a more harmonious working environment between student and teacher.

Body positive

Do you know what impact body language can have in the classroom? You probably haven't really given it a great deal of thought, but the effective use of body language is one of the most powerful tools in any successful teacher's toolkit.

As humans we are aware of the nuances in a person's body language almost instinctively. Some people radiate charisma and others annoy us even though we can't put our finger on what it is we find unsettling about them. Often this is because we are detecting and decoding minute aspects of their behaviour and demeanour which give away their true intentions even if they are not actually voicing them explicitly. This is never truer than in the classroom environment where as a teacher you are being minutely regarded by your students. There is research which suggests that we make our mind up about an individual in the first five minutes of meeting them.

What tips are there for managing your own body language effectively to motivate students, diffuse conflict and make them think that you are always the self-assured and knowledgeable teacher you aspire to be? Act confidently. You may be quaking inside or perhaps are reluctant to teach your Year 8 horrors. However you mustn't let the students pick up on this. Easier said than done, so what can you do?

- Get to the class early and greet students firmly at the door.

- Smile. Make brief eye contact with your students. Show your students that you are pleased to see them and that you are looking forward to getting through a lot in today's lesson.

- Command the attention of the class from the start by walking into the centre at the front and beginning the lesson assertively. State the lesson's objectives clearly.

- Use open hand gestures such as raising your palms upwards and spreading them out to include the class and to show them they will be actively involved in the lesson.

- Open body language is much better than closed body language; crossed arms give a signal that you are angry, nervous or defensive.

- Avoid talking loudly over students; dramatic pauses and looking pointedly in the direction of any students chatting is much more effective than trying to outcompete them or worse, shrieking at them at high pitch.

- Be aware of barriers. Giving instructions while hidden behind piles of books on your desk signals low confidence and a lack of authority. Sometimes it will be appropriate to take time at your desk to support individual students, but to give yourself maximum authority stand at the front and centre of the room to address the class.

- Include all the class in your vision. Be aware that there will be side pockets of the classroom where you may not always look. You need to make a conscious effort to draw in all students. This is particularly important if students are observing a demonstration in PE or Science or watching a video. Students who hang back or those not in direct view will lose focus and drift off.

- Pace the room. Don't stay rooted to the spot. Roam. If you are reading or explaining something to students feel free to walk to the back of the room. Observe the classroom from there. Can you see what you have written on the board?

- Standing near chatterers or those off task is often enough to rein them in. If the students know you are always rooted to a very small space by your desk, then the back of your classroom may provide a haven for whisperers and daydreamers. Show students that the classroom is your environment and that you are at ease in it.

- Use non-verbal signals as a highly effective way of reminding students what they should be doing. Quick, brief, repeated gestures are an effective way of getting students to amend their uniform without verbally nagging them or getting into a dispute. Miming pulling off a jacket can indicate that a student needs to remove their coat or pointing repeatedly at your neck signals that a tie or top button needs doing up.

- Speak to students at their level by bending down when helping them with their work. It can be intimidating and a barrier if you are looming above them. Ensure you can still see the rest of the class by standing to their side. It is not a wise idea to have your back to the rest of the class.

- Even if you are telling off a student, avoid close face-to-face confrontation and do not shake your finger at them. Instead try to use calm body language and remember that giving the student a minute or so to calm down and then having word with them by the classroom door can diffuse a situation. Avoid creating a dramatic scene in public and making the student lose face with their peers.

- Be aware of your body language around the school. You may need to swagger a bit to get into the lunch queue if you are a young teacher (I got sent to the back several times as dinner ladies thought I was a sixth former!). Greet or at least smile briefly at the students you teach when you see them around school.

- Stride the corridors and look purposeful. Not only will this keep you fit, but the students will know you mean business when they first see you and this will ease the process when you come to teach them on a cover lesson. First impressions are important, so take a deep breath, smile and radiate confidence and quiet authority.

Phrasing it positively can make all the difference

Have you considered how the words you choose are crucial in engaging students – getting them to do what you want, building their confidence and fostering a positive classroom climate?

Have you ever noticed the way successful teachers interact with students? Of course you see it every day. But do you really listen to what they say and how they say it? Teachers who have excellent relationships with their students and who are able to get the most truculent teenager to respond to their requests and work hard in their lessons seem to have a secret, special knack. Wouldn't you like to know what it is?

If you analyse these teachers' responses to students you will find that they usually stress the positive and phrase things in such a way that students are keen to respond. Not sure? Well read these tips from amazing teachers and see how you can learn to get a positive vibe in your classroom – and get even surly Simon and sulky Chantelle to respond to your requests with a smile.

Firstly, think of someone at school or that you have worked with recently that you would do anything for. No, I don't mean the gorgeous French assistant or the sexy new Science teacher! Think of someone in authority who inspires you. Perhaps it is your head of department, deputy or, if you are lucky enough, head teacher or other senior member of staff. What is it about the way they act and respond that means you are willing to go the extra mile for them? You know, do an extra cover when it is not your turn or do something awkward and unpleasant such as an extra lunch duty or swapping detention supervision – anything that doesn't directly benefit you and where you could easily avoid doing it. Most people have a surprisingly limited number of people that they would really put themselves out for at any great inconvenience. But there are a select few people that you would be prepared to walk over hot coals for, and this is true for students as well as teachers. It is not always immediately obvious why these charismatic individuals inspire such devotion, but I am sure you can think of plenty of individuals in your staffroom or beyond that don't inspire you in this way.

Jo, a current head of department, remembers her previous boss. 'She was great. Completely positive at all times and really made me believe that I was capable of being a great deputy head.' But what was it that made her so positive? 'Every time I suggested something, even if I thought it sounded stupid, she would question me a bit and then say: "Great: you can do it. It will be fine!" This constant positive reinforcement really made me feel that I could do more and try out new things: that it would work out fine, or that if it went wrong at least I had her support.' Now as a head of department, Jo tries to instil this positive approach with her colleagues – with the result that all of her team are motivated and keen to take imaginative risks with their teaching.

Secondly, be upbeat and use positive language in the classroom. Some weaker students find it easier to refuse to work at all rather than risk the chance of failure. Be aware that students may also feel threatened by a blank sheet of paper, an examination paper or a whole novel and will refuse to cooperate. Build a supportive climate in your lessons by making students feel they can achieve by praising them before they start a task:

- Refer to previous success (e.g. 'You did really well on the Romans and you can tackle this project using the skills you learnt.').

- Break down large, frightening-looking tasks into bite-size chunks (e.g. 'Let's focus on the opening of your essay first.').

- Refer to tasks as 'getting started' or 'getting on' rather than 'work', which can sound negative.

- Refer to the behaviour you would like to see. Phrase it in a positive way. 'Let's get on quietly' is much more positive than 'Stop talking!'

- Treat the students in a positive and respectful way. They really do notice and it develops mutual respect. In the heat of lessons it can be tempting to yell 'Shut up!' or 'You are the worst class I have ever taught!' This is always a mistake. Students respect teachers who keep calm, even when they are being rude and unpleasant. It is much easier to say, 'I treat you with respect' if you actually do. Students take their lead from the teacher and although you may be seething inside, take a deep breath and keep calm. One of the biggest gripes students have is with teachers who deal with them badly or who don't seem to be interested in teaching them. They always notice if you treat them like an adult, and everybody prefers to be reasoned with rather than shouted at.

- Talk to students in a way that suggests that you are expecting their compliance (e.g. 'Thank you for picking up that crisp packet' or 'Thank you for taking your coat off'). This is a highly effective way of getting students to act in the way you would like and gets them on your side. Quite often they will have responded before they have really processed what they have done.

- Use students' names and make them realise that you know them as individuals and that you like them. Make an effort to smile and use eye contact when you see them around school. Use duty time or even detentions as opportunities to get to know your students better and take an interest in them. Ask questions and take an interest in their answers. Refer to successes they are having in your lessons (e.g. 'I really enjoyed your homework: your dragon-slaying elf story was really gripping!'). These interactions outside the classroom are really important for building relationships in the classroom.

- How you use praise is vital in cultivating the sort of classroom where students work harmoniously and where they will be willing to go the extra mile for you. Think back to the last time when you received praise for something. It is a fantastic feeling and one of the biggest motivators there is. Increase the amount of praise you use by a ratio of five to one and be prepared to be amazed!

Thinking point

- What three thoughts have you had from this chapter?

- What three tiny targets are you going to plan and try out in your lessons?

In the next month, in my lessons I will trial out:

1.

2.

3.

Reflection moment

- How did it go?
- What worked?
- What could have gone better?
- What would you try again?

Chapter 15

Dealing with Difficult Classes

Sometimes however amazing you want to be there is a particularly tricky class that seems to get you down. Although all of the advice in this book is relevant for dealing with the really difficult class, it is common to feel that a particular group is causing so many problems that they deserve their own chapter.

In my first year of teaching I thought all Year 8s were hellish. I'd had a horrible group during teaching practice and now I had the dreaded Year 8T. They were literally the class from hell. How do you know when you've got a class from hell and more importantly what can you do about it? Several seasoned teachers offer their advice below about how they deal with their most troublesome classes.

It is important to recognise that all students, even the very bright and usually very well behaved, have the potential to turn unpleasant on occasion so it is important that you are putting into place all the strategies you can and are not overlooking your role in managing behaviour. Teacher Michelle Graeme explains: 'Last year most of my classes were great, but I had a low set Year 9 German class. They knew they weren't going to be taking it as an option and couldn't be bothered. They would muck about and roll up my worksheets and generally chuck stuff about. In the end I spent less and less time preparing their lessons. I felt really angry with them; if they couldn't be bothered then neither could I. Unfortunately this meant their behaviour got worse and worse.'

Although it is natural to feel as if you are wasting your efforts on planning good lessons for such a class, once you think like this then things will only degenerate. It is not unusual to want to lavish more care, time and exciting resources on your 'favourite' classes, usually *über* keen Year 7s or top set GCSEs, but this will only serve to make them keener and your naughty class even less motivated.

Step 1: Make them your priority

The first step in dealing with ACFH (A Class from Hell) is to make them your priority, at least until you get their behaviour cracked. Resist the temptation to leave their lesson planning until last and really think about what strategies you can use to get them focused and engaged with the task. It is natural to want to loiter in the staffroom until the last possible moment before getting to the class, but getting to the classroom first and greeting the students at the door makes a real difference.

Georghia recalls: 'I had this class last year I really didn't get on with. They were a top set GCSE class and this made things worse. I think I was meant to feel honoured to be given them, but actually lots of the girls were really bitchy and critical. Nobody would answer any questions and I felt totally at sea.' Eventually things came to a head when she was observed by her mentor: 'I thought the lesson had gone reasonably well, but it had been really tense and the students had been completely unresponsive.' Expecting her mentor to be sympathetic she was surprised by her reaction, 'She said to me, "You really don't like that class much do you?" I was so shocked and she was so right.' Her mentor explained that it was obvious to the class that Georghia didn't like them and as a result they refused to cooperate with her. 'I did manage to change things eventually,' she added. 'I've learnt that however much you may hate a class it is important *never ever* to let them know it. It is almost as if you have to put on an act, and pretend you are pleased to see them – even if you are not. I also learnt to give a bit more praise and start seeing the class as individuals. When I really broke it down, the whole class wasn't bitchy – just two tables of girls. I broke up their group and found that by praising individuals the atmosphere in the class changed completely. Not overnight, but by the end of the term, I actually found that I wasn't actually having to pretend to be pleased to see them – I genuinely was!'

Thinking point

So how do you know if you've got a class from hell? Do you ever:

- Find yourself hoping that a fire alarm / training day / act of God will mean you don't have to teach them?
- Dread the days that you've got that class?
- Talk about the class so much that your partner / friend / parents know about the dreaded 8T?
- Feel crushed / angry / completely depressed after your lessons with them?
- Worry about somebody else seeing you (try to) teach them?

- Leave their marking/planning until the last minute – they can't be bothered, so why should you?

Step 2: Cover your bases – remember the tried and tested methods

- Make them your priority for lesson planning and marking for at least a couple of weeks.
- Check the SEN register. Have any of them got special educational needs that you need to be aware of? Check their individual action plans and ask the SENCO for advice. Maybe Robbie is acting up so much because he can't hear when sitting at the back and should be at the front?
- Take control of the classroom. Get to it before them. Meet and greet them.
- You decide on the seating plan. Split up troublesome groups. The initial battle is worth the long-term gain.
- Get them started quickly. Have something focused for them to do as soon as they enter the room.
- Reinforce verbal instructions with written instructions on the board.
- Make the purpose of the work very clear. Many students don't want to do the work because they can't see why they are doing it. Share the big picture and if you can give them choices or tie in the work to their interests then consider this.

- Look for the positives. Praise the students who are cooperating.

- Be aware of the school discipline policy. Keep to it.

- Give warnings and stage your punishments. Give students a chance to respond and modify their behaviour. 'Jenny, if you carry on chatting with Toni then I'll have to move you to that seat on your own. So if you continue talking you'll be moved. This is your final warning,' is much better than erupting: 'Jenny. Move now!' This type of response means it is likely she'll refuse, argue or walk out.

- Give students choices and allow them to save face. Don't be confrontational for the sake of it. Give students a get-out clause rather than demanding they act straightaway: 'Oh dear. I'm going to have to confiscate those amazing earrings unless they disappear in five seconds, four, three . . .'

- Mean what you say and do what you mean. Giving punishments is a last resort but if you set a detention or punishment then follow it through. Students soon suss who is a pushover.

- Find things to praise. Some classes never have praise. Give them a noticeboard to display their best work.

- Give students roles in the class. Students who feel they have a responsibility for giving out the books / cleaning the board / filling out the merit board can be praised and therefore feel valued.

- Be consistent. Philip throwing some paper at Jenny might be the last straw for you, but if he is punished unfairly – unlike the rest of them who have also been throwing paper – you'll be seen as unjust. (It is the thing students hate most in a teacher.)

- Don't hold grudges. Expect the best from them and start each lesson as if they will behave. Never say, 'I don't want you to act in the awful way you did last lesson'; this is only reminding and reinforcing bad behaviour.

- Don't ever really lose your temper. It is necessary to pretend you are very cross sometimes, but once you feel your blood boiling for real, the taken a step back.

Thinking point

If the above sounds familiar what three things are you going to try to turn around in this class and improve their attitude? Remember, breaking long-established patterns of behaviour (yours and theirs) will take a determined effort – but it will be worth it.

If you have asked a student to stand outside the classroom, return after break, etc. to discuss his/her behaviour, explain that everyone has a choice and every choice they make has a consequence. Whether it is completing work to a high standard and the consequence is praise, or behaving in a manner where the consequence is to call home or invite the parents in to discuss the poor behaviour. They must remember every choice they make results in a consequence!

Rebecca Garvin-Elliot, Roade School, Northampton

Three things I will do to improve attitudes to learning in my class:
1.
2.
3.

Stage 3: Look at things differently and try new tactics

Okay, so you've tried all of the above. It still doesn't work. You've slaved all weekend over their lesson plans but you are still struggling to get silence. They really are the class from hell. Don't despair . . .

- Ask to observe a colleague in another subject teach them. Hopefully you'll see them use some really good techniques that you can use or you'll see that they are not perfect with them either.

- If *all* the other teachers say the class are a 'nightmare' then you really shouldn't have to teach them without using the school's behaviour support system. Explain to your head of department or senior leadership team that you need some help to succeed with this class. If this is not possible then make sure you relentlessly use the behaviour systems available in your school. If you can identify the ringleaders then refer their actions through the school system. Don't be afraid to ask for help and insist on support. Getting individuals on a report system or involving senior teachers isn't an act of weakness; it shows that you are refusing to allow a minority of students spoil your lessons.

- Speak up. As a teacher you will get some challenging classes. However, if you are finding a class really tough to crack then your line manager would prefer to hear the concerns from you rather than get a complaint from a student's parent or overhear World War III through your classroom walls.

- Share your concerns and ask for an observation: 'I'm finding my Year 8 class really tough. I've planned this to do with them . . . Would you mind looking over my plan?' This gives others a chance to help you if you've set something inappropriate and may also give you a chance for some valuable reflection. Then if it still goes badly: 'I was wondering if you'd come into my Year 8 class. I'm finding them really challenging and I'd welcome some tips . . .' They may well act like little angels because your bulldog of a head of department is present but at least this will give you the chance to praise them and let them experience a good lesson. You can always ask your colleague to pop in during the next lesson.

- Talk over your experiences with other teachers and don't be afraid to ask for advice. Remember, everybody has challenging classes at one time or another; it is how to respond to the challenge that matters.

Chapter 16

Dealing with Difficult People

An amazing teacher sometimes has to deal with difficult people and they can be a barrier when you want to get on and do your job. Hopefully the difficult people you encounter will be few and far between but it is inevitable that you will meet some at some stage.

Difficult people usually fall into one of the following groups: pupils, parents, other teachers and line managers. Most people really want the same results regardless which group they are in. They want pupils to achieve, enjoy their lessons and not to cause them any trouble. That is true whether you are Neal Smith from 11TW who doesn't complete the homework you set, the despairing Mrs Smith (mother of Neil) you telephone, your colleague or the head of department in charge of discipline.

Please refer to chapter 15 on dealing with difficult classes and it is worth remembering that, although some pupils appear not to care and aren't bothered by your lessons, punishments or rewards, most of them do want to feel that their teacher cares about them and wants them to succeed. The teenage ego is a very fragile one; much bravado and bluster covers up the fact that these young people often feel very uncertain, fearful of failure and choose to behave obnoxiously or arrogantly to cover this up. An amazing teacher keeps persisting with these pupils and through consistency and determination eventually wins through.

Dealing with difficult parents

Difficult parents though can be another matter! Sometimes parents' evenings can be a revelation and you begin to have a little more sympathy for Neal, and see *just* why he's turned out the way he has, when you meet his parents. There's a whole spectrum of issues when dealing with parents from the *very* pushy middle-class parent who thinks their child is much more intelligent than they are, to the parent who is in despair because they cannot manage their child's wilful adolescence. The following tips are worth bearing in mind because they serve well in a variety of situations.

Number 1: Be informed and keep parents regularly updated

One parents' evening, in my early years of teaching, I launched into a full explanation of the failings of one particular girl in my classes. She was naughty, loud and rude. After my rant, which consisted mainly of how loud she was and the fact she didn't listen, the parent looked at me coldly and remarked: 'You really should have known that Chantelle is partially deaf in one ear!' Now, Chantelle still had behaviour and attitude issues, but as you can imagine the fact that I wasn't aware of this information made me feel absolutely terrible. It also annoyed her parents (which meant that they refused to take on board *any* of my criticisms when in fact some of them were relevant and just). In their eyes *I* had not done *my* homework properly and therefore the problem was all mine! This was an unpleasant experience, but I learnt from it and always made sure that I researched pupils thoroughly and was very aware of any SEN, medical or family issues before contacting parents. It meant too that I was better aware of and catered for all my pupils' needs. So, when dealing with parents you need to make sure you know all of your facts, making sure that your own behaviour and how you deal with the child in the classroom isn't exacerbating the situation.

Additionally, you need to keep parents regularly updated. It is always an error to 'store up' material for parents' evenings. If there are any gradual or growing problems then it is important to have signalled these much earlier either to the tutor or, depending on your school, to the parents themselves. Storing things up until they are a large and unyielding bundle does nobody any favours. By making regular early contact with home as soon as difficulties occur you give yourself and the parents a chance to resolve them. You are also giving the parents some forewarning about what to expect. Most importantly you have demonstrated that, by using your time and making the effort for the phone call, you care. All of us in life would rather receive difficult information at an early stage because this is when issues are less of a problem and there is a better sense that we are able to do something about them.

Number 2: Show you care

Many of the conflicts with parents centre on the fact that as a teacher you are telling them that you find their children difficult to deal with or just plain lazy. The large majority of phone calls home I have had to make as a head of department centre on the fact that there is poor behaviour in class, or much more frequently that the pupil hasn't completed homework or classroom work either at all, or to the best of their abilities.

One of the things I have found most effective is to stay absolutely calm and have the clear belief that you are on the same side. Sometimes when I am in school I hear teachers talking on the phone to parents recounting their child's misdeeds. Naturally when you are relating them you can become quite heated and almost re-live the experience including the sense of anger and outrage. It is really important that it is not transferred across to the parent in that way. If it is then this is when it becomes the start of a battle between the parents taking the side of the child ('yes I can see why you think Mrs Jones is a moaning old . . .') and the teacher seeing the parent as part of the difficulty instead of an ally in reforming the child's behaviour and getting things back on a positive footing.

One of the most important phrases I ever use in my conversations with parents, either directly or indirectly, is that the reason I'm ringing them, requesting that Neal serves yet *another* detention, is because *I care.* If you can get this across you will find it has an amazing effect; parents will magically allow children to attend homework or revision sessions and it can soften even the hardest of hearts. For many, parenthood must be a terribly disappointing and depressing experience – some of them receive several phone calls a week about their children's misbehaviour. If you can get across the message that you are ringing because you care and that there's a chance that Neal will pass English GCSE or whatever it is then you are much more likely to succeed in winning the parents' goodwill.

Number 3: Don't forget to share the good news as well as the bad

As teachers we are very quick to act when children meet our low expectations – when homework isn't complete, when deadlines are missed or when behaviour is below par. How often do we pick up the phone to share good news? Now I'm not suggesting that you do this all the time – it would be an incredible drain on time. However, in changing behaviours and managing people better one of the best things you can do is to thank them and praise them when they have done something well. So the next time one of your naughtier or less reliable pupils completes some good homework, scores well in a test or whatever the success might be, make sure that their parents know about it. This of course also serves for all pupils – we need to be much quicker to praise if we want to really see results.

I taught a very bright but troublesome boy for GCSE; after much effort (largely nagging from me and some good talent from him) he completed an outstanding GCSE folder of coursework. Although I had had plenty of contact with his parents previous to this, regarding late work, poor behaviour and detentions, I decided in a spare five minutes to ring up and relate some good news for a change. It was the best thing I could have done. His mother was so shocked and surprised at receiving in her words ('the only positive phone call I have ever had about him in fifteen years') that she burst into tears. Importantly I had a firm ally (when in later months I needed to contact her about less pleasant things, she was more than willing to lend her support). As for the boy, the praise he received at home as a result of my phone call improved our relationship and he worked much harder in class. Although phone calls are a nice personal touch, don't forget a similar effect can be achieved by noting down positive comments in the homework planner or by using 'praise postcards' or whichever reward system your school uses to inform parents about good behaviour, attitudes and work.

Number 4: Make appropriate use of evidence

Things have a tendency to get fraught when we discuss things and make statements at parents' evening that appear to be value judgements. Comments such as 'Chloe doesn't appear to be working hard enough or taking her studies seriously,' might be a very fair and true reflection of her working style, however because it is very opinionated it can be easily disputed or taken personally *by parents.*

When having difficult discussions with parents, try and show them examples and hard evidence in a non confrontational and judgemental way. Make sure you don't try and blind them with jargon and 'education speak', something that fills many parents with confusion, fear or irritation. For example, if Chloe isn't working hard enough and looks like she is underachieving, explain to them that she has the ability and *potential* (a very powerful word to use in getting parents on your side) to get a Grade B, but that unfortunately she is only working currently at a Grade D level. Then show some of her work at this level, indicating how it could be improved; this is likely to get a much better response than just criticism. This is because it will offer a clear explanation, and one that appears more constructive because there is evidence (the work on show) combined with the use of the grades. Many parents have told me that they feel at a loss to *know* what to do when a teacher shares concerns with them – sometimes you can't provide easy answers, but in this case showing the work followed up with clear advice makes the next steps a bit clearer.

Number 5: Think about what you would like the outcome to be

This is an important factor when dealing with any difficult individual or situation. Remaining focused on what you want the desired outcome to be means that you can try and take the personal out of the situation and focus more constructively on a solution. When dealing with difficult situations there can be the temptation to indulge in blame and lots of circular discussion about what has happened and where the fault lies. In order to resolve situations and move things on, try and think about what you want the resolution to be. Try and deal with it in these terms. Phrases that signal that you are looking forward such as 'our next steps', 'what would help' and 'what we need to do next' help focus on an outcome because they lead to a resolution.

Dealing with difficult members of staff and line managers

Most of the colleagues and people who manage you are likely to be a cause of joy and delight in your professional life. I have worked with many thousands of pleasant, intelligent, friendly, fun, creative and giving teachers. These have enhanced my life and helped my teaching expertise – I have become a better teacher because of their ideas, their help, their positive 'can do' attitudes and their friendship. However it is also true that the very tiny number of people who I have found 'difficult' have caused me a disproportionate amount of stress. This can impact on your ability to be an amazing teacher and do what we know is an amazing job.

This is a book about how to be an amazing teacher – not how to deal with people or problems but some tips for dealing with tricky troublemakers may come in handy. If however your concerns are more serious and you find you are having persistent or serious problems with a particular individual or feel that you may be being bullied then you need to make sure you seek guidance from managers in your school or your union.

Avoid negativity

Many people are keen, enthusiastic and positive. When you met these people it rubs off on you, you feel lighter, happier and life has more possibilities. Negative people have the opposite effect, but be warned their moods and attitudes are much more contagious. Avoid the 'drainers' those people that lurk in the staff room filled with ennui, counting off the days until they retire (I have seen it done – on one really sad occasion, even calculating the number of hours left teaching! This is someone who really should have just handed in her notice. Can you imagine being in her classes?) These drainers have one joy which is sniping at those who enjoy their job and trying to bring down their enthusiasm.

These 'drainers' can bring down your mood even when you feel at your best, and they can be much more harmful when you are having the occasional bad day or lesson, as they can make you feel that everything is *always* like this even when it isn't. Where you have a choice try and avoid them – I am not suggesting that you become unfriendly just seek out those who lift your spirits rather than those who try and drain them. It is important to do this because our energy and enthusiasm is affected by those with whom we have most contact. When you do have contact with those who are pessimistic listen to what they say, but avoid getting drawn in to long over blown debates; instead maintain your own positive stance.

Bear in mind the motivation behind some colleagues' difficult or prickly manner. They might be envious or resentful of your teaching success. They may be struggling with a difficult Year 8 group that you find an absolute delight to teach and your comments about this class can provoke feelings of inadequacy. Pupils can be brutal in telling a less effective teacher than 'Mrs Smith' they had last year for Maths 'was so much better than you and her lessons were *amazing*.' There is not a great deal you can do about this; you need to be aware and recognise the motivation behind some people's attempts to undermine your success. This will explain why some are very opposed (without good reason) to a new idea or teaching technique you are proposing.

Obviously we all have difficult days and times when things don't go so well for us. It is *how* we manage these setbacks that determine whether our day is a disaster or a success. An amazing teacher aims to be positive so that pupils, staff and parents find their interactions enjoyable.

Thinking point

Who are the most positive people in your school? What is it about them that radiates this enthusiasm? How do they act? What can we learn from them?

Practise good communication

Most conflicts stem from poor communication and misunderstanding. Often we are too busy thinking about what *we* want to say next, or how something will affect *us* to really listen to what the other person is trying to communicate. Practise the art of really listening to the other person, try and rephrase things back to them to check you have understood what they are trying to tell you: 'are you saying that . . .' or 'Can I just check that I have understood you correctly?' Make sure you have really understood what they are trying to say before you jump in. If we all did this and took a little more time to listen many errors and conflicts stemming from misunderstandings would cease. That doesn't mean to say that you have to agree with or even like what the other person has said – but it does mean that you have shown them the courtesy of listening to what they have said in the first place.

If you need to have a conversation about something that is likely to be difficult or sensitive then pick your time carefully. Think about where you are having the conversation and make sure it is private and cannot be overheard by other staff or pupils. If it helps you to think about what you are going to say then it can be useful to jot down some notes, although be aware if *you* are the line manager then this can make the conversation seem much more formal and serious. This may not be the impression you wish to create. However if you are meeting your head teacher to discuss *your* increased workload some notes will help you ensure that what you are saying is factual and that you do not forget anything.

What's in it for me?

Some people are giving and generous with their time and efforts, some will go out of their way to help you. These people do not cause you difficulty – they enhance your life and realise that a little give and take goes a long way. Difficult people are often difficult because they are too centred on the 'what's in it for *me*?' in any given situation. Whatever situation you are in, trying to understand the viewpoint and perspective of the other person is a helpful first step to making progress with that relationship.

People who are just concerned with themselves can be difficult to deal with because an appeal to their generosity of spirit fails. You need to think carefully about what motivates them – whether it is your Line Manager who just wants an easy life and simple solutions or a new colleague who doesn't want to pull their weight in the planning of the new scheme of work and wants you to do it all for them. Once you have worked out what their motivation is, and of course there can be a whole range, try tapping into this in dealing with the problems and the solutions you offer.

The line manager above may not be your best bet for a sympathetic ear and as someone to help you think through and decide what to do in a given situation – you will need to enlist the help of someone else for this. However they are likely to respond positively to any practical strategies that you suggest – *if* they solve the problem. You can use this knowledge to your benefit. Likewise with your work-shy member of department, suggest that you will offer her some good lesson plans *if* she commits to providing some in return. This is more likely to appeal to her nature, which expects useful transactions rather than the willing giving of favours.

When you are asking people to do things you do need to be aware of the 'what's in it for me?' mentality. Perhaps we should stop and think before we ask people to do things to consider how it will help them or improve things. We really need to do this in order to get people on board with what we want them to do. People can be particularly 'difficult' when they feel that they are stressed or are being overloaded by colleagues or more usually their line manager or head teacher. If they feel overworked and sense that you are further overburdening them then you are likely to meet with resistance. This is when you need to play the 'what's in it for me?' card, by encouraging them that doing whatever it is in *their* best interests even if that interest will only be realised further down the line. For example, a line manager managed to encourage a colleague to collate their resources into a helpful scheme of work. He did this by persuading them that in the long run it would save them time, and as it was his area of responsibility people would be able to find the resources in a convenient central place, rather than keep pestering him and asking him to explain and find them for him. Being persuaded that time invested *now* would benefit him later was the best way of motivating him.

When discussing new ideas and systems with people who might be difficult it is important to really think about what you want to achieve. Have things organised, well thought out and clearly in place; this will help your confidence when you present them with things they may not want to do.

How do you treat people?

In your own behaviour make sure that you aren't too much 'what's in it for me?' Give a little and take a little. Remember we are all irritated by those people in life who only contact us if they want us to do something for them: make sure that you put some deposits in your goodwill bank before you try and make any withdrawals. You can't expect people to do favours for you or treat you particularly well if you don't do the same for them.

One way of dealing with people who are often difficult or resistant to ideas is to do them a favour and try to sometimes make life easier for them. This way of behaving in itself can often be effective since people who are habitually difficult can often alienate other individuals and by doing them the occasional favour you create a depository of goodwill that you can draw on.

Even if people remain defiantly difficult the way you treat them is very important. It can be too easy to fall into the trap of disliking *them* and treating them as if they are just a problem. Difficult people will have unlikeable *characteristics* but it is very important to separate these from the person – treating them in the same way that you would any other individual; sometimes by doing this it is possible to actually win that person over.

Reflection moment

Think about a situation that included difficult people which you successfully resolved. What skills did you choose? Why were you effective?

Which of the strategies above do you use most frequently? Are there any other strategies or thoughts that you think you might be able to employ when facing difficult behaviour?

Record two of these strategies here:

1.

2.

Chapter 17

Lifestyle Management: Time Management and Workload

Teaching can be a very pressurised job. Many teachers can suffer from feelings of stress and the sense of being overwhelmed by the daily demands made on them. When this happens you lose the enjoyment you get from teaching and your skills can slip – being *amazing* appears to demand too much effort. Unfortunately many of the generic books on stress and lifestyle management suggest tips and strategies that are not applicable or practical to teaching. For example, in a recent article published for newly qualified teachers it advises not working outside school hours citing: 'If you do find yourself working through the holidays or outside school during the week, you may quickly become tired and stressed, which will have an impact on your personal well-being.' (Stanley, 2010) In fact it gives no helpful tips about how to avoid this. This is because with teaching *some* evening and *some* holiday working is *necessary*. It is finding appropriate ways to manage this, striking a balance between your working, social and personal life wherein lies the answer to managing workload and enjoying your life.

So how does an amazing teacher manage their stress and keep themselves fresh and resilient in the face of the different pressures and demands the job makes? This is achieved firstly by managing their *work-life balance*. An amazing teacher adopts some practical steps to help organise their life. They realise the following are helpful in making the best use of their time at school and at home:

1. **Forward planning and careful long-term lesson planning**

> Medium-term planning is important because it helps you to chart your way through a busy term. Detailed planning for individual lessons is not the best use of time if as a result you turn up to lessons tired. Value creative spontaneity over dogmatic planning. Whether learners learn is important and not the militaristic nature of your planning.
>
> Russell Carey, Head of Department, Yorkshire ❞

The amazing teacher knows that it is important to have a long-term view of what all their different classes will be doing. They know that it is important to manage assignments, tasks and reports so that they won't all be due in at the same time. They plan a good variety of lessons for their class – so that while their GCSE class might be working towards a hefty written assignment that might require many hours of hard marking, their Year 8 class is working in groups on oral presentations that will be delivered and marked by verbal comment in class. The amazing teacher knows that while maintaining and planning this overview may take thirty minutes of their time each week, being prepared, they feel less stressed because they know what they are doing. It also provides valuable 'air pockets' and breathing spaces between different groups' marking demands. They realise that not all learning needs to be assessed by a full written outcome and by managing a range of group, verbal and written activities this provides variety and interest for the class as well as avoiding a marking overload.

The amazing teacher thinks carefully about the homework they set and, because of this forethought, they do not automatically set mountains of writing work under the mistaken assumption that this is the only way that good learning happens. Homework demands effort from pupils but includes a good variety of learning, investigation and reading homework. These tasks help the pupils learn but do not increase the teacher's marking workload. Please have another look at chapter 9 Helpful Hints for Homework if you need some further inspiration in managing this important aspect.

At home

The amazing teacher uses the same diary or recording mechanism for home and social appointments as for school. This means that they are easily seen and held in one central place. They frequently review what is happening ahead of each week so that they can forward plan and make sure that key social events or pressure points are noted and planned for well in advance. They put into place a range of simple forward-planning strategies, for example, having a regular stock of birthday cards, stamps and generic gifts to avoid frantic last-minute dashes to the shop. This overview means that they are less likely to forget and be caught out by events, and if they are, they have some resources to help deal with them.

2. Different forms of assessment

The amazing teacher knows how to use peer- and self-assessment. They realise that time is well spent training up their classes on how to comment and reflect upon each others' work. This means that they are skilled at commenting on each others' work and that the adoption of regular peer- and self-assessment lightens their marking load, helps with lesson planning and importantly skills up pupils so that they know what they need to do to make their work better. If you feel that you are not adopting these strategies and would like further guidance on this please refer to Section II: Assessment for Learning and the Amazing Teacher.

At home

The amazing teacher carries on with the philosophy of skilling up individuals in the way they treat their family and friends. The aim should be to create independence and to use the expertise of others – particularly if you have the tendency to take on everything yourself. Encouraging other family members to contribute to the smooth running of the family home will ultimately reap rewards for them as well as you. Yes, like Year 8, they may need training and their first efforts will not be as good as your own, but persevere and they will help share the load, leaving you time to focus on the parts of running a home that you are most effective at or that you enjoy most. If you are single, paying people to do specific jobs that you dislike such as window cleaning, gardening, car washing or ironing is not being lazy. It allows you to focus on what you would rather be doing and gives you more leisure time helping you to manage your time better and become a happier more effective teacher.

3. Making time for yourself!

The workload of a teacher is infinite; don't try to get it all done. Aim to do your best and work efficiently but also make time for yourself.

Ian Kirby, Roade School and Sports College
Northamptonshire ”

The amazing teacher appreciates that with teaching some evening, weekend and holiday working will be necessary. They realise that it is unrealistic to fit everything into the school day – work *will* need marking, lessons *do* need preparing and reports *will* need writing. However, the amazing teacher manages their time effectively and ensures the best result for them.

They keep a careful eye on deadlines and plan their work accordingly. They know *when* they work best: whether they are an owl or a lark. Some of the most effective teachers I know work in a very focused fashion: one head of sixth form I knew always got into work an hour early every day and would accomplish all of his marking in this time. When he was at school early in the morning, he benefited from the quiet environment and the fact that the photocopier and resource room would be at his disposal. He felt at his freshest before the rigours of the day had started. This was much more effective for him than trying to complete work at the end of the day when he would have a constant stream of people waiting to see him about sixth form matters.

Other staff manage their work by staying at school until a specific time, say 5 o'clock, and do not take anything home with them, thereby leaving the evening free for relaxation and domestic activities. Others need to leave school promptly for child care issues and then pick up work later in the evening: it does not matter what you do as long as whatever you do works well for you. What I would advise against though is time wasting. Spending lots of time aimlessly sorting things, feeling as though you ought to be working, sitting at your desk, getting very little done but finding that another evening has passed you by. This does not help lessen your workload or help reduce stress; instead you have a feeling of being constantly busy and confined by work but you actually achieve very little indeed.

Keeping focused

Amazing teachers work in a very focused fashion, *if* they are working they are working. This then allows them to have time off in the week and enjoy other pastimes whatever they may be. Once, when I was training middle managers, I met a very lively, enthusiastic head of maths. Many of the middle managers on the training course had been complaining that they did not have any time for a social life: work was seeping into all areas of their life. This particular teacher had lots of energy and enthusiasm. When I asked her what her secret was she said that every Wednesday evening she went out for sushi with another teaching friend! They allowed themselves a 10-minute cathartic discussion about school, but then moved onto other things or watched a film at the cinema. She said that knowing that she had this regular, enjoyable social commitment each week meant that she worked particularly hard after school on Mondays and Tuesdays knowing she would have some time off. Importantly, she commented that the ability to have some dedicated fun time off was worth the effort. Personally the thought of sushi leaves me cold, but the learning point is there; deciding *when* you are going to work effectively is important, as is keeping some parameters and deciding when you will have time off.

It is important to have time for fun and relaxation for yourself. An amazing teacher is one who is rested and refreshed and meets their classes with optimism and enjoyment. There will always be too much to get done in teaching, but it is important to earmark some quality time for yourself to do whatever you enjoy doing whether that is a sport, catching up with a friend or even eating raw fish! You need to have moments of joy and time in the week to call your own, so that you will feel happier and more effective working hard at other times.

School holidays aren't just time for rest and relaxation. This is of course very important; however, there will inevitably be some schoolwork that needs to be done. You need to acknowledge this and then decide what works best for you. Most effective teachers keep a central list of things that need doing – when they reach a holiday such as a half term they decide *before* they get to the break which day or days they will use to get their schoolwork done. This sort of forward planning means that you will actually enjoy your time off and you will still get the jobs done that you need to do.

Work-life balance advice that advises you to 'not work at all in holidays' or weekend or evenings is not very effective for a teacher at all – in fact such advice can create further stress. Not planning lessons properly, letting marking pile up to mountain height, not dealing with an ever increasing 'to do list' and trying to relax about it just creates further stress, difficult lessons and criticism from senior staff. One of the best ways of managing workload is taking steps to plan and tackle jobs, making sure that there are clear parameters between 'working' and rest time.

4. **Choose your time and know when you work best**

You know when you work best. Experiment with different working patterns and then plan out a timetable. One thing that can cause a lot of worry and distress is the constant feeling that you should be doing something and it hangs over you blighting your free time.

You know how it is when you start the weekend aware that you need to make a start on your Year 10 reports, but you don't actually get started and your Friday night, Saturday and Sunday feel tainted by this feeling. In the back of your mind is a little voice nagging: '*You should be writing your reports.*' Instead take control and make a firm appointment with yourself – decide that you are going to spend an hour and a half writing them at 5pm on Sunday – and then don't worry about it until then. Taking control, planning your time and making decisions means that you can enjoy your leisure time without feeling that undone work is always casting a black shadow over your day.

Diary management

Treat time with yourself as you would any other appointment. Write it down in your diary – perhaps using a different colour pen. If you don't allocate time and people ask you if you could just supervise that detention, attend that meeting in their place or mind their child then it is difficult to say no, especially if they see you have an empty slot in your diary. Writing things down makes you feel that you have made a firm commitment to yourself: so ring-fence that time off. Make sure you are allowing yourself some time to do some activities that help you relax and enjoy yourself. By doing this you are not neglecting your teaching duties – there is always too much to get done as a teacher – what you are doing is focusing your working time and allowing for some inner refreshment which will make you a more imaginative, happier and better teacher.

Think about which tasks you do demand most concentration and energy. Marking AS Level mock papers demands that you are focused and razor sharp so that you are not making errors: it demands some real thought. The same often goes for writing schemes of work or looking at data. Plan challenging tasks like these that demand high-level thinking for when you are fresh. Some tasks demand little brain work – sorting out your resources and some administrative tasks can be done when you are feeling more tired or need to give yourself a bit of a break: make sure you do these less challenging tasks when you need a lull perhaps at the end of a busy day, rather than wasting serious 'brain time' on them.

5. **Make good use of administrative support**

If you have a tutor group or manage a department think about investing a small amount of time into developing some 'pupil monitors' who might be able to help with some low-level tasks like sorting resources, designing wall displays etc. This can help pupils take responsibility, learn new skills and help them develop better relationships with staff. It will take a little time training them and some rewards or other incentives, but it can be very useful if you find yourself completing lots of low-level tasks – wishing you had eight pairs of arms. Make sure you are also making full use of any administrative assistants your school has so that you are not undertaking unnecessary, burdensome work yourself.

6. **Prioritize your time and focus on what really matters**

Don't take on too much as it may compromise the standards of what you do!

Robert Francis, Examiner, teacher and trainer ”

One of the things that causes the most stress in schools, is the feeling that there is never enough time to get everything done. School days can feel fairly relentless; at the end of every lesson there is another set of pupils all waiting to hear your words of wisdom and then another. Lunchtimes, breaks and after school can be swallowed up with optional clubs, duties and activities. Think carefully with your classes and your role as a teacher about what *the most important things* are. Focus on them. It is good to get involved in school events and run extracurricular activities, but beware of taking on too much. It is important to keep the balance right.

Once you are seen as very keen and effective (skills of an amazing teacher) there can be a danger that *everybody* will want you to get involved with *everything.* Of course this can be very flattering but be aware you only have so much energy and time in your resources: *if* you spread yourself too thinly your classroom teaching, energy and enthusiasm will suffer. Even if you are trying to build a particular career path with your teaching, if you are always taking on new things make sure you are prepared to pass on some things otherwise your burden can become unwieldy. Sometimes if you have done a task – say editing the school newspaper for a couple of years – then actually you have gained all you are going to out of it and it is time to try something else. Make sure if you are always taking on new things that you do leave some things behind. One of the key things in managing stress is keeping some control over what you choose to do and making sure you do not choose to do too much.

Try to take on new challenges every couple of years: Key Stage co-ordinator; G & T leader; Mentor etc. New challenges keep teaching 'fresh' although try not to hold the post for too long otherwise it could become stagnant.

Rebecca Garvin-Elliot, Roade School and Sports College ”

7. Deal with the things that are causing you stress

One of the best ways of managing stress is to take action against the things that are creating stress for you. Obviously a certain amount of stress and pressure is healthy, without it we would not feel the urgency to get things done and a certain about of stress gives us the 'boost' to perform well when, for example, we are teaching and being observed, on interview or meeting the in-laws! This sort of stress helps us reach our potential. However, if you are beginning to lie awake at night worrying, or you start suffering aches and pains or you start acting differently, for example, becoming more irritable or bursting into tears on a regular basis, then these are signs that you might be suffering from stress.

Obviously, if you feel that you are under a great deal of pressure it is important to contact your GP. Often before things get too difficult we would be wise to take some preventive action. If you feel that your workload is too heavy, or that some classes or individuals in them are making your life a misery, then you should ask for some time with your line manager so that you can discuss this with them and start implemening some useful strategies. Battling with some individuals in classes that regularly display poor behaviour, or feeling swamped by burdensome tasks can lead to feeling overwhelmed. Sometimes it is helpful to make notes about what it is about the situation that is causing you distress and what you think could be done to help resolve matters. Sometimes conflicts occur between individual staff and pupils and 'timeout' from being in the same lesson can be helpful. If you feel consumed by your overall workload, keeping a record charting what you are spending your time doing and for how long can help pinpoint where your time is spent and provide a helpful basis for discussion.

One of the most helpful things you can do when you are feeling tense or stressed is to think about taking some action to help address the issue. Often the first step in doing this is talking to another person, whether it is a friend, fellow professional or your line manager.

8. Developing effective relationships

Teaching is a social job. You interact with pupils and staff for most of the day. Obviously, sometimes it is these very interactions themselves that are the causes of stress. Please do work through the strategies for 'Dealing with Difficult Classes' in chapter 15 for managing difficult students and if it is tricky staff or line managers making your life feel fraught then make sure you follow the advice in chapter 16.

Developing positive relationships with other staff can be one of the great joys of teaching. I am still in close contact with a fellow NQT from my very early days of teaching back in the 1990s. Developing good relationships with other staff is one way of 'stress proofing' your life and adding enjoyment to your school days. It is essential to find teachers who you can share a joke with, let off steam with and provide each other with mutual support in the day-to-day business of school life. A little laughter and a shared joke can go a long way to making difficult days seem more bearable and help make moments of tension evaporate.

In order to be involved and included in school and non-school social events make sure you take some of your breaks in the school staff room. It can be all too easy to stay holed up in your own classroom, but you will miss out. Get to know and appreciate your colleagues, make friends and take up social invitations that interest you. Schools that have this sort of camaraderie are more enjoyable places to work – staff are happier coming to school. Social networks and happy working environments are important.

Things I have seen in happy 'friendly' schools include things such as staff lunches, (each Friday individuals bringing a different item of food or drink to share and mark the end of the week in a friendly, convivial fashion) cinema and theatre clubs where staff sign up to watch something of interest and go for a drink afterwards, even such simple things as magazine and book-swopping boxes (and a nice way to recycle your reading material, receiving something 'fresh' and 'free' to read in return). Even just the agreement to go to the staff room on a particular day, taking your lunch for a chat and a proper rest, can be a really positive way of making your day so much better. If events like these do not happen at your school, find a like-minded chum and start something off – even if it just starts with a couple of you, you will find that things will start to grow and you will develop wider supportive networks.

Developing strong networks of friends in work and at home is one of the best ways of stress proofing your life and making it more enjoyable. Moreover keeping up with a like-minded group of individuals allows you ready access into a social life and ways of sharing and exchanging tips and ideas that will help you in the day-to-day experience of school. Knowing that you have peers in school that you can rely on, laugh with and who are happy to see you makes work an altogether more enjoyable experience.

9. Get organised!

One thing that can cause a lot of stress and distress is wasted time looking for things that are mislaid at home or at school. In dealing with your work-life balance it is a good idea to adopt the habits of somebody you know who appears to be very organised and who has things well under control.

Strategies that I have seen used to good effect include: keeping a to-do list so you can see what you have achieved and what you have still to do; keeping and filing things efficiently, for example, including a 'current folder' for all those things that you have just been given but know that you will misplace; when opening your post try and immediately action things – this will mean that you never have to pay interest on an outstanding credit card bill – throwing away things immediately if you will not use them, and set up an efficient filing system for those things that you know will come in useful but not for a few months.

Effective people know that it is the *outcome* that really matters, not how it is achieved. There are no special awards for creating lessons, schemes of work or tests from scratch. Make good use of the internet, teaching and subject associations. Make sure you share good ideas with colleagues and develop helpful networks with teachers from other schools. An organised teacher knows where to find and file resources that they have used in previous years and they aren't afraid to adopt or adapt resources from the internet, from colleagues or other schools. They are organised in that they know where the best resources are located and they keep careful records enabling them to write reports and solve problems quickly and efficiently. Organised teachers have systems and they use them; they allow time to plan what they are going to do and this means that they have more time to be creative and play!

Seek advice from those who are successful

No one benefits if you work yourself to exhaustion. You also have a life and the essential energy which makes you a good teacher flows from that.

Alan Wiggins, teacher at Birmingham City University and Inspector

Finally, look at those people in school who manage their life well. They are calm, organised and successful and importantly they enjoy the job. What habits and tips can you find out from them? What teaching and behaviour strategies do they have for managing tricky classes? I was immensely flattered as a head of department when a NQT in another subject asked if she could observe me as apparently I handled her tricky GCSE class really well in my lessons. Did I mind? Not a bit! The NQT said she learnt many strategies which she would immediately use in her lessons. When I was learning my craft I did not do this often enough.

If I had my time again, I would certainly ask people for some of their tips to lighten my load, so I could benefit from their experience rather than learning the hard way. Managing the work-life balance can be tricky at times – that is why they call it a balance – and yes, experience really helps. You begin to recognise the pressure points in the year and plan for them accordingly. But there is nothing to say that you can't find a few short cuts on the way by learning and emulating others' good advice in this book and beyond.

Thinking point

Look again at the ten different strategies for managing a work-life balance above.

For each one, give yourself a mark out of 5. Give 5 if you think you follow that advice fully, down to 1 if you think you are lacking in this area.

- Which areas are you most successful in?
- Which areas do you most need to concentrate on?

Reflection moment

What are the three things you are going to do in the next ten days to improve this area. Remember to try and make them SMART (specific, measurable, achievable, relevant and time-specific) targets. So 'having more time to myself next week' is too vague but 'Going to the staff room for lunch on Wednesday' and 'going to a yoga class after school on Friday' is specific enough.

List the three things, record the date and review your progress after ten days.
1.
2.
3.
Progress:
Date:
Successes:
Areas for improvement:

Chapter 18

Keeping Yourself Fresh and Interested

Teaching is a marathon not a sprint. School terms are intense and arduous; amazing teachers want to enjoy their career over the long term. Some of the tips below will be helpful in ensuring you get the most out of your teaching and personal life. It is very important to keep your own enthusiasm levels high so that you remain keen about your career choice and continue to enthuse the young people with whom you work every day.

In order to maintain a positive enthusiastic approach it is important to do things that fuel your interest in the subject you are teaching. Teaching is by nature a very giving career, but there can be a danger that you neglect the passion that brought you into the job in the first place. Robert Francis, an English examiner and teacher, reminds us that in his subject teachers must:

> Keep reading literature for yourself, as it is easy to let this slip when you are marking what seems like thousands of books each year. ”

This is true whatever your subject. You need to do things that inspire you and that relight and deepen your appreciation for whatever it is you are teaching. Sometimes you might not have time to do this until the holidays but you should be on the lookout for ways to feed your passion. It is important to do things that get you really excited, for example: Art teachers should visit galleries and explore new artists, musicians play in a band or attend concerts and English teachers should see plays and experiment with their own writing skills – you get the picture!

Thinking Point

Have a think – what is it that most excites you about the subject you are teaching?

If you had some spare time how would you wish to use it?

What new books, research or ideas are there in your field or area of expertise that you might like to read?

Have you recently heard an expert or attended a training course in your subject?

Reflection moment

Take five minutes to think of the things that you would like to do to enhance your love of teaching and enjoyment of your subject, if you had the time.

Record them below; if there are more feel free to really go for it and record them.

1.

2.

3.

4.

5.

Next, go through the list and plan over the next six months when you might be able to tick one of these off your list. Look out for events, articles, people and projects that might help you. Remember that sometimes items on your list can probably be linked to your own professional development and training. It may be possible for funding to be linked to this; it is always worth asking your school CPD co-ordinator whether this is the case.

When did you last learn something?

After a few years of teaching it can be all too easy to get into a rut using the same approaches and teaching the same topics in the same way. It is important sometimes to put ourselves in the role of a learner and experience something new, different or unusual. While we may not use that particular experience in our own teaching we are awakening our curiosity and this in turn makes us open to new ideas. We have all come into teaching because we have an urge to share our knowledge about a subject, and because we feel that we have a particular area of expertise to share. Renewing and recharging this is very important in keeping us keen, interested and excited by what we are teaching.

Sometimes our interest and enthusiasm can be developed from learning more about the assessment, qualifications or subject knowledge we teach. Russell Carey a head of department in West Yorkshire reminds us that:

> Getting involved in some activity (e.g. examining or delivering training to other teachers) keeps your subject expertise fresh and up-to-date. An occasional day away from school (on such legitimate business) can help you to retain a proper perspective on things. ”

Finally, we should do things just because we want to and not because they are connected with our subject at all. Sometimes these can yield the greatest benefits. Perhaps there is something you have always wanted to learn, try or achieve? Perhaps you think you haven't got enough time. Think again. In my fourth year of teaching a colleague and I attended an 8 week aromatherapy and massage course on a Wednesday night. This had nothing to do with my schoolwork, although it was held at my school. For an hour and a half once a week we experimented with oils, laughed and listened as we were taught by a skilful aromatherapist.

This experience was thoroughly enjoyable, in no way connected with my job, but I did benefit from listening to someone else teach, and taking part in something practical that was so very different from my day-to-day job. It was so very nice being the pupil for once, with no responsibility, no lesson plans, just the willingness to learn and have fun! My friends that year undertook a wide range of fun courses just to do that, these included: wine tasting, French lessons and belly dancing. Most importantly they were doing something that they found fun and interesting. This led to them feeling excited and enthused about themselves and they brought this into their classroom.

So what's stopping you becoming an amazing teacher? You've read the book and taken on board plenty of advice and useful tips. But remember the joy of teaching is that although amazing teachers share many similar character traits, no two teachers are exactly alike. It's up to you to experiment, try out and tackle some of the advice that you have found useful and make it your own. You can't hope to exactly replicate somebody else's teaching – but you can experiment and develop your own highly successful style! You are on your journey to becoming an amazing teacher – enjoy the ride and let me know how it turns out for you.

About Caroline Bentley-Davies

For more information about other books, training, or speaking engagements or to discuss *How to become an Amazing Teacher,* training or INSET day at your school or college, you can email her at:

caroline@bentley-davies.co.uk or visit
www.bentley-davies.co.uk

Caroline runs a wide variety of training courses for teachers through Osiris Educational www.osiriseducational.co.uk and Lighthouse training www.lighthouse.co.uk

Further reading and resources

Alexander, Jane. *The Five Minute Healer: A Busy Person's Guide to Vitality and Energy All Day, Every Day* (Gaia Books, 2000).

Allen, Lynette. *Behind with the Marking and Plagued by Nits: Life Coaching Strategies for Busy Teachers* (Crown House Publishing, 2006).

Assessment Reform Group. *Assessment for Learning: 10 Principles – Research-Based Principles to Guide Classroom Practice* (Assessment Reform Group, 2002). Available at www.assessment-reform-group.org/publications.html (accessed 10 March 2010).

Black, Paul and Wiliam, Dylan. *Inside the Black Box: Raising Standards through Classroom Assessment* (NFER Nelson, 2004).

Black, Paul, et al. *Assessment for Learning: Putting it into Practice* (Open University Press, 2003).

Ginnis, Paul. *The Teacher's Toolkit: Raise Classroom Achievement with Strategies for Every Learner* (Crown House Publishing, 2001).

Hook, Peter and Vass, Andy. *The Behaviour Management Pocketbook* (Teachers' Pocketbooks, 2004).

Marland, Michael. *The Craft of the Classroom: A Survival Guide* (Heinemann, 1975).

Rogers, Bill. *You Know the Fair Rule: Strategies for Making the Hard Job of Discipline in Schools Easier* (Prentice Hall, 1997).

Stanley, Julian. Under Pressure. *The Times Educational Supplement* (2010, 15 January).

Swainston, Tony. *Behaviour Management* (Network Continuum Education, 2007).

Thomas, Will and Hailstone, Phil. *Managing Workload Pocketbook* (Teachers' Pocketbooks, 2005).

www.teachersupportnetwork.co.uk – a useful website and phone line dealing with a range of teachers' issues and concerns.

Index

A

B

C

D

E

F

G

T

U